Grammar Inquiries, Grades 6–12

In this book, grammar expert Sean Ruday shows you how to apply the principles of inquiry-based learning to improve your grammar instruction.

Grammar often gets relegated to worksheets or rote tasks, but with this volume you'll find a wealth of strategies and tools for making grammar instruction engaging and meaningful.

Designed for middle- and high-school ELA teachers, this book covers all aspects of grammar instruction through an asset-based approach and includes many methods, ideas, and takeaways for instruction. Featuring real-world examples of student work and a sample lesson plan, this is an essential resource for teachers who wish to enliven instruction and teach grammar effectively.

Sean Ruday is Professor and Program Coordinator of English Education at Longwood University, the Co-President of the Assembly for the Teaching of English Grammar, and the Founding Editor of the *Journal of Literacy Innovation*. He writes and presents on innovative literacy instruction. This is his 17th book.

Also Available from Routledge Eye On Education
(www.routledge.com/k-12)

The Early Elementary Grammar Toolkit
Using Mentor Texts to Teach Grammar and Writing in Grades K-2
Sean Ruday and Kasey Haddock

Remote Teaching and Learning in the Elementary ELA Classroom
Instructional Strategies and Best Practices
Sean Ruday and Taylor M. Jacobson

The Elementary School Grammar Toolkit, Second Edition Using Mentor Texts to Teach Standards-Based Language and Grammar in Grades 3–5
Sean Ruday

The Middle School Grammar Toolkit, Second Edition Using Mentor Texts to Teach Standards-Based Language and Grammar in Grades 6–8
Sean Ruday

Inquiry-Based Literature Instruction in the 6–12 Classroom: A Hands-on Guide for Deeper Learning
Sean Ruday and Katie Caprino

The Multimedia Writing Toolkit Helping Students Incorporate Graphics and Videos for Authentic Purposes, Grades 3–8
Sean Ruday

The Informational Writing Toolkit Using Mentor Texts in Grades 3–5
Sean Ruday

The Argument Writing Toolkit Using Mentor Texts in Grades 6–8
Sean Ruday

The Narrative Writing Toolkit Using Mentor Texts in Grades 3–8
Sean Ruday

The First-Year English Teacher's Guidebook Strategies for Success
Sean Ruday

Culturally Relevant Teaching in the English Language Arts Classroom
Sean Ruday

Grammar Inquiries, Grades 6–12

An Inquiry- and Asset-Based Approach to Grammar Instruction

Sean Ruday

Taylor & Francis Group
NEW YORK AND LONDON

Designed cover image: © Getty Images

First published 2024
by Routledge
605 Third Avenue, New York, NY 10158

and by Routledge
4 Park Square, Milton Park, Abingdon, Oxon, OX14 4RN

Routledge is an imprint of the Taylor & Francis Group, an informa business

© 2024 Sean Ruday

The right of Sean Ruday to be identified as author of this work has been asserted in accordance with sections 77 and 78 of the Copyright, Designs and Patents Act 1988.

All rights reserved. The purchase of this copyright material confers the right on the purchasing institution to photocopy pages which bear the photocopy icon and copyright line at the bottom of the page. No other parts of this book may be reprinted or reproduced or utilised in any form or by any electronic, mechanical, or other means, now known or hereafter invented, including photocopying and recording, or in any information storage or retrieval system, without permission in writing from the publishers.

Trademark notice: Product or corporate names may be trademarks or registered trademarks, and are used only for identification and explanation without intent to infringe.

ISBN: 978-1-032-54314-7 (hbk)
ISBN: 978-1-032-54257-7 (pbk)
ISBN: 978-1-003-42426-0 (ebk)

DOI: 10.4324/9781003424260

Typeset in Palatino
by SPi Technologies India Pvt Ltd (Straive)

Contents

List of Figures	vi
Meet the Author	viii
Preface	ix
Acknowledgements	x
Introduction: Using Students' Inquiries and Assets in Grammar Instruction	1
1 Building the Foundation for Inquiry-Based and Asset-Focused Grammar Instruction	10
2 Showing Students Examples of Authentically Used Grammatical Concepts	25
3 Reflecting with Students on the Importance of Authentically Used Grammatical Concepts	37
4 Helping Students Identify and Analyze Authentic Examples of Grammatical Concepts	52
5 Creating Opportunities for Students to Share Their Findings	66
6 Asking Students to Reflect on Their Experiences	81
7 Assessing Students' Work on Their Grammar Inquiries	96
8 Implementing This Approach: Suggestions for Classroom Practice	113
Conclusion: Why Inquiry- and Asset-Based Grammar Instruction Makes a Difference	128
References	133
Appendix A: A Guide for Book Studies	135
Appendix B: Reproducible Charts and Forms to Use in Your Classroom	142

Figures

Figure 1.1	Subordinate Clause Grammar Inquiry Description	14
Figure 1.2	Mentor Text Analysis Graphic Organizer	21
Figure 1.3	Infographic–Building the Foundation for Inquiry-Based Grammar Instruction	24
Figure 2.1	Some Texts Where We Can Find Grammatical Concepts in Our Everyday Lives	26
Figure 2.2	Graphic Organizer: Examples and Features of Grammatical Concepts	34
Figure 2.3	Infographic—Showing Students Examples of Authentically Used Grammatical Concepts	36
Figure 3.1	Grammatical Concept Discussion Graphic Organizer	49
Figure 3.2	Infographic—Reflecting with Students on Grammatical Concepts	51
Figure 4.1	Grammatical Concept Analysis Graphic Organizer	55
Figure 4.2	Infographic—Helping Students Identify and Analyze Authentic Examples of Grammatical Concepts	65
Figure 5.1	Grammar Inquiry Presentation Flyer Example	68
Figure 5.2	Grammar Inquiry Presentation Guidelines Example	70
Figure 5.3	Student Presentation Example: Strong Verb Analysis	73
Figure 5.4	Student Presentation Example: Subordinate Clause Analysis	75
Figure 5.5	Infographic—Creating Opportunities for Students to Share Their Findings	80
Figure 6.1	Strong Verb Reflection Example	85
Figure 6.2	Subordinate Clause Reflection Example	86
Figure 6.3	Reflection Question One Brainstorm Template	90
Figure 6.4	Reflection Question Two Brainstorm Template	91
Figure 6.5	Reflection Guidelines Example	92
Figure 6.6	Infographic—Asking Students to Reflect on Their Experiences	95
Figure 7.1	Grammar Inquiry Rubric	99
Figure 7.2	Example Grammar Inquiry Rubric: Seventh Grade	104
Figure 7.3	Example Grammar Inquiry Rubric: Tenth Grade	106
Figure 7.4	Infographic—Assessing Students' Work on Their Grammar Inquiries	112

Figure 8.1	Example Lesson Plan One	115
Figure 8.2	Example Lesson Plan Two	117
Figure 8.3	Example Lesson Plan Three	120
Figure 8.4	Example Lesson Plan Four	123
Figure 8.5	Example Lesson Plan Five	125

Meet the Author

Sean Ruday is Professor and Program Coordinator of English Education at Longwood University and a former classroom teacher. He began his teaching career at a public school in Brooklyn, NY, and has taught English and language arts at public and private schools in New York, Massachusetts, and Virginia. He holds a BA from Boston College, an MA from New York University, and a PhD from the University of Virginia. Sean is the founding editor of the *Journal of Literacy Innovation* and the co-president of the Assembly for the Teaching of English Grammar. Some publications in which his works have appeared are *Issues in Teacher Education*, *Journal of Teaching Writing*, *Journal of Language and Literacy Education*, and *Contemporary Issues in Technology and Teacher Education*. He frequently writes and presents on innovative ways to improve students' literacy learning. You can follow Sean on Twitter at @SeanRuday and on Instagram at seanrudayliteracy. In addition, you can learn more about Sean's work on his website, www.seanruday.weebly.com. This is Sean's 17th book with Routledge Eye on Education.

Preface

Grammar is all around us. As an English education professor and literacy professional developer focused on the most effective practices of grammar instruction, I have developed a deep understanding of the way that grammar functions as an essential tool for all aspects of communication. Grammatical concepts are certainly present in the books that we and our students read (both in and outside of school), but they do not stop there. The purposeful and strategic use of grammar is central to all forms of communication: text messages, social media posts, podcasts, song lyrics, dialogue in films and shows, magazine articles, website information, sports broadcasts, and so much more. In my work, I talk about grammar with a variety of audiences and stakeholders: I conduct professional development workshops for teachers, I give conference presentations, I teach college courses on grammar instruction, and I work with elementary-, middle-, and high-school students to help them understand grammar. In all of these contexts, I emphasize the idea that grammar does not just exist in textbooks and on worksheets: it is a key part of the way we communicate in authentic situations. By thinking about grammar in this way, we are able to understand grammar more deeply and work with it in engaging and relevant ways.

This book is based on the idea that grammatical concepts are important tools for authentic communication. It connects the idea of authentic language use to inquiry-based learning, in which students use "big picture" essential questions to guide and support their learning experiences. In the inquiry-based approach to grammar instruction described in this book, students look for authentic examples of grammatical concepts in their out-of-school lives, analyze the importance of those concepts to the contexts in which they're used, share their insights, and reflect on the experiences. Through my research, study, and instruction on grammar, it has become clear to me that an especially effective way to help students learn about grammatical concepts is to create space for them to examine the central role those concepts play in their real-world experiences with language. This book is designed to give you the skills, tools, and information to help your students engage in meaningful grammar inquiries that center their identities and experiences while also facilitating their deep analyses of the importance of key grammatical concepts. I am delighted that you have chosen to study grammar inquiries, and I would love to communicate further with you about the ideas in this book.

Acknowledgments

I want to thank everyone at Routledge Eye on Education for their insight, guidance, and support. I am thankful for the opportunity to work with such a wonderful publisher.

I am extremely appreciative of the outstanding students with whom I worked on these grammar inquiries.

I would like to thank my parents, Bob and Joyce Ruday. I am grateful for their encouragement in all aspects of my life.

Finally, I want to thank my wife, Clare Ruday, for the happiness she brings to my life.

Introduction

Using Students' Inquiries and Assets in Grammar Instruction

The seventh-grade English classroom was packed. Family members, caregivers, and community members stood in the back of the room or brought in extra chairs from the media center to see the students share the results of their grammar inquiries. Another English teacher brought her class so that they could both support their fellow students and learn from them: the students in that class were about to engage in grammar inquiries of their own. Before the first student gave a presentation, I addressed the entire class in a huddle that looked like something before a sporting event. "You all have worked so hard and done such an amazing job," I gushed. "Be proud of everything you've done. Also, have fun today. Everyone here is so excited to learn from you."

On this day, the seventh-grade English students with whom I worked were giving what we called grammar inquiry presentations. These students had recently been studying the grammatical concept of prepositional phrases. After they learned about the key features of this concept and its importance to effective writing, the students began grammar inquiries focused on prepositional phrases. To do this, they identified examples of prepositional phrases they found in their out-of-school lives and analyzed the importance of those prepositional phrases to the contexts in which they were used. The students then prepared presentations on the examples they identified, the contexts in which they were used, and the significance of those examples to those contexts. These presentations were what the audience had gathered to see.

To the delight of the standing-room-only crowd, the seventh graders' grammar inquiry presentations were excellent—they were varied, innovative, and insightful. Through their work, the students shared instances of prepositional phrase use in situations such as video game strategy discussions, the lyrics of popular songs, social media posts, directions to local destinations, sports broadcasts, their own creative writing, everyday conversations, and more. One student explained,

> I realized that I use so many prepositional phrases when I'm playing video games with my friends and we're giving each other advice about what to do and where to go. We're always saying things like 'past the barrier,' 'over the wall, and 'on your left.' This project helped me understand why prepositional phrases are important and how much I use them.

After the students shared their insights in their presentations, the crowd roared in appreciation of their outstanding work. I addressed the students again, exclaiming "You all showed such great understandings of prepositional phrases and taught us all so much. Your inquiries were fantastic!"

Taking An Inquiry-Based Approach to Grammar Instruction

This description of a seventh-grade English class sharing the results of their grammar inquiries provides an introductory example of how this approach to grammar instruction can look in action. Now that we've taken a first look at this classroom example, let's delve more deeply into what it looks like to take an inquiry-based approach to grammar instruction. We'll do this by first exploring what inquiry-based learning is and then considering how it can relate to grammar instruction.

What Is Inquiry-Based Learning?

Inquiry-based learning is a pedagogical approach that uses meaningful questions, real-world connections, and authentic applications to engage students in in-depth learning experiences. To engage in meaningful inquiry, students investigate thought-provoking questions that reflect complex and interesting topics (Lee, 2012). This approach has become popular in education because of the way it centers students in the curriculum and aligns with in-depth thinking. When working on a challenging and meaningful inquiry, students cannot look up specific answers online and then be finished—they must think in complex and multifaceted ways about an idea about which they would like to know more, ask questions that address this information, and investigate that question.

The kind of question that aligns especially well with inquiry-based learning is called an essential question, which Wiggins and McTighe (2005) define as "A question that lies at the heart of a subject or a curriculum (as opposed to either being trivial or leading), and promotes inquiry and uncoverage of a subject" (p. 342). These questions are thought-provoking, "big-picture" questions that go beyond factual recall and facilitate students' deep learning and understanding. McTighe and Wiggins (2013) assert that an essential question possesses most or all of the following characteristics. Such a question:

- Is open-ended;
- Is thought-provoking;
- Calls for higher-order thinking;
- Points toward important, transferable ideas;
- Raises additional questions and sparks further inquiry;
- Requires support and justification, not just an answer;
- And recurs over time, or can be revisited frequently.

(p. 3)

By investigating questions that contain these attributes, students can experience the agency, relevance, motivation, and learning benefits that inquiry-based learning provides. Inquiry-based approaches to learning that center authentic questions and real-world applications have been applied to a variety of subject areas, but its connection to grammar is a new concept. In the next section, we'll begin to explore how inquiry-based learning can align with effective and engaging grammar instruction.

How Can Inquiry-Based Learning Relate to Grammar Instruction?

Inquiry-based learning has the ability to maximize the effectiveness, relevance, and authenticity of grammar instruction. While grammar instruction has traditionally not been associated with relevant and authentic work, focusing instead on out-of-context worksheets (Weaver, 1998), inquiry-based grammar instruction provides a student-centered alternative to this. In the inquiry-based approach to grammar instruction described in this book, students look for authentic examples of grammatical concepts in their out-of-school lives, analyze the importance of those concepts to the contexts in which they're used, share their insights, and reflect on the experiences.

These inquiries align with essential questions about the importance of grammatical concepts to authentic, out-of-school communication in students' lives. For example, the students in the example discussed at the beginning of this chapter focused on the essential question "How are prepositional phrases important to the communication in our everyday lives?" when engaging in their inquiry. Similarly, when those same seventh graders examined the concept of strong verbs later in the school year, they considered the essential question "How do strong verbs make the texts we encounter outside of school as effective as possible?" By examining questions such as these, students can engage in meaningful inquiries that address ideas and topics related to authentic applications of grammar instruction. Through these inquiries, students do more than memorize grammatical terms and complete out-of-context activities—they find authentic uses of grammatical concepts and consider the importance of those concepts to the real-world situations in which they exist. These opportunities for real-world identifications and analyses help students develop deep understandings of the role of these grammatical concepts in effective communication.

Rooted in Culturally Relevant and Sustaining Teaching

The inquiry-based and student-centered approach to grammar instruction described in this book has its roots in the culturally relevant (Ladson-Billings, 1995) and culturally sustaining (Paris, 2012) teaching and learning. Through the culturally relevant and culturally sustaining educational practices that Ladson-Billings and Paris respectively describe, teachers create learning environments that value, incorporate, and center students' cultures and identities. In culturally relevant pedagogy, "teachers utilize students' cultures as a vehicle for learning" (Ladson-Billings, 1995, p. 161) through three important and related practices:

- Students experience academic success
- Students develop and/or maintain cultural competence through learning activities that affirm their identities
- Students develop a critical consciousness that helps them think critically about the world around them.

Grammar inquiries are designed to align with each of these principles—as students investigate authentic uses of grammatical concepts in their out-of-school lives, they learn important content, which helps them experience academic success, and they incorporate their identities and experiences into the classroom in relevant ways, which corresponds with developing and/or maintaining cultural competence through learning activities. In addition, grammar inquiries align perfectly with opportunities for students to reflect on the experience by considering what they learned from identifying and analyzing real-world examples of a grammatical concept and why what they learned from this authentic experience is important. These reflections on students' experiences, what they learned, and why that knowledge is significant aligns with the idea of developing a critical consciousness. It helps them think critically about the value of engaging with authentic examples of grammatical concepts and how this work emphasizes the significance of these concepts to their real-world experiences with language. (This reflective practice is described in more detail in Chapter 6: Asking Students to Reflect on Their Experiences.)

Similarly, students who engage in grammar inquiries learn about grammar in culturally sustaining ways. According to Paris (2012), "culturally sustaining pedagogy seeks to perpetuate and foster—to sustain—linguistic, literate, and cultural pluralism as part of the democratic project of schooling" (p. 93). The culturally sustaining teaching and learning that Paris describes "embrace cultural pluralism and cultural equality" (p. 93). By looking at examples of grammatical concepts in their out-of-school lives, students participate in grammar instruction that values a variety of ways of using and applying these concepts. Instead of seeing grammar instruction and usage in out-of-context ways that are disengaged from their lives and communities, inquiry-based grammar instruction approaches grammatical concepts as tools that play important roles in students' authentic lived experiences.

The Significance of Students' Assets

The inquiry-based approach to grammar instruction I describe in this book aligns with asset-based instruction, which approaches teaching, learning, and assessment in ways that focus on real-world connections to classroom material and meaningful applications of students' knowledge (New York University, 2020). In an asset-based approach to instruction, teachers "decenter themselves while centering their students through opportunities to show what they know and can do in authentic and relevant ways" (Ruday & Caprino, 2022, p. 4). Conversely, deficit-based approaches to teaching and learning focus primarily on factual recall and out-of-context activities without regard for meaningful connections, authentic applications, and students' real-world experiences. The 2020 piece "An Asset-Based Approach to Education: What It Is and Why It Matters," published by New York University's Steinhardt School of Education, explains that an asset-based approach is important to building an inclusive and equitable classroom: "It seeks to eliminate deficit thinking and harmful biases that hold back students, especially those with disabilities, English language learners and emergent bilinguals, and students of color" (para. 7). Teachers who see students' cultures and backgrounds as assets can create relevant and inclusive learning environments that help them succeed in supportive learning environments (Milner, 2011).

The inquiry-based grammar work described in this book applies the ideas of asset-based teaching and learning to grammar instruction: it helps students see grammar instruction as an opportunity to apply their knowledge of grammatical concepts to authentic communication in their communities and out-of-school contexts. In contrast, deficit-based grammar instruction focuses solely on factual recall of abstract concepts with no authentic connections and does not incorporate the language-related knowledge and experiences that students already bring to the classroom. Inquiry-based and asset-focused grammar instruction goes beyond this way of thinking by centering students' authentic experiences in the curriculum and privileging the unique and personal ways they can study and investigate real-world uses of grammatical concepts. For example, when students examine uses of grammatical ideas such as strong verbs and prepositional phrases in their real-world contexts, their academic work connects with their out-of-school experiences. In addition, this instructional approach communicates to students that the ways that use and engage with language are important to the grammar activities they do in school. They are not just in school for someone else to teach them about grammar—they are instead there to apply their knowledge in meaningful and relevant ways. By reenvisioning grammar through an asset-based approach, we educators can maximize students' agency and create a space that values the assets they bring to the classroom.

Why I Decided to Write This Book

I wrote this book to provide middle- and high-school English language arts teachers with a resource that can help them engage their students with grammar in thought-provoking, culturally relevant (Ladson-Billings, 1995), and culturally sustaining (Paris, 2012) ways. The book is designed for educators who are interested in using inquiry to help students deepen their understandings of the grammatical concepts through student-centered instructional methods that incorporate students' assets. While there are other resources that relate to inquiry-based teaching and learning (Wiggins & McTighe, 2005; McTighe & Wiggins, 2013; Ruday & Caprino, 2020), no professional book written for teachers applies this framework specifically to grammar instruction. Given that it can be particularly challenging to engage students in grammar in meaningful ways (Ruday, 2020c; Weaver, 1998), I believe that this book can be especially useful for teachers as they seek ways to teach grammar as effectively as possible.

I have been working with students on inquiry-based grammar instruction in recent years, sharing ideas through shorter articles on the topic

(Ruday, 2020a; Ruday, 2020b), and have noticed outstanding results with this approach. In my experiences supporting students through inquiry-based work on grammatical concepts, I have been impressed by their engagement with the work, the curiosity they've applied to these inquiries, their thoughtful reflection on the significance of the grammatical concepts they've found in their out-of-school lives, and the pride they've taken in sharing relevant examples of grammatical concepts to their classmates and community members. I am excited to share ideas, resources, insights, and suggestions with you, the educators who are reading this book and learning new methods of meaningful grammar instruction.

What to Expect in This Book

In this book, you'll find a step-by-step guide for incorporating inquiry- and asset-based grammar instruction into your middle- or high-school English language arts classroom. Chapters 1 through 7 of the book each discuss an important part of the process of implementing this approach to teaching and learning grammar in the middle and high school English classroom. Chapter 1 describes how teachers can build a foundation for inquiry-based and asset-focused grammar instruction, using mini-lessons and mentor texts to help students understand key aspects of grammatical concepts and understand their importance to effective communication. Chapter 2 begins to delve deeper into inquiry-based grammar instruction by discussing ways for teachers to model for their students the identification of authentically used grammatical concepts they find in their out-of-school lives. Then, Chapter 3 expands on this work with suggestions for teachers to follow as they work with their students to identify the importance of the authentically used concepts they identified.

The book's next three chapters discuss in detail how teachers can support students as they engage in their own inquiries. The ideas in Chapter 4 provide recommendations for teachers to follow as they help their students identify examples of grammatical concepts in their out-of-school lives and analyze the importance of those examples to the contexts in which they're used. In Chapter 5, we'll look at ways to create opportunities for students to share the findings from their grammar inquiries with peers, caregivers, and community members; this practice provides students with authentic situations in which they can celebrate their inquiry results. Chapter 6 describes ways that teachers can help students reflect on their experiences with grammar inquiry with questions and activities designed to promote students' metacognition of their learning and their awareness of the importance of making connections between concepts they learn in school and their out-of-school lives. Next, Chapter 7, discusses suggestions for assessing students' work on their grammar inquiries. This chapter describes key assessment principles associated with this work to consider as well as sample assessment descriptions and rubrics.

For consistency and ease of use, Chapters 1 through 7 are divided into the following sections:

- *What Is It?* This section describes the chapter's key concept, discussing key concepts and familiarizing readers with important information that will help them understand the chapter's focus.
- *Why Is It Important?* This section makes a case for the importance of the chapter's focal concept, explaining why the information presented in the chapter plays a key role in inquiry-based grammar instruction.
- *How Can It Look in Action?* In this section, I'll share examples of my work in the middle- and high-school English classroom related to this concept. These sections draw on my experiences working with seventh- and tenth-grade English classes on inquiry-based grammar instruction. We'll see how the seventh graders engaged in grammar inquiries on strong verbs and how the tenth graders worked on inquiries addressing subordinate clauses. In each chapter, I share descriptions of my work with these classes and how I supported the students as they engaged in grammar inquiries.
- *Instructional Recommendations.* In this part of the chapter, I provide key instructional suggestions for teachers to keep in mind while putting the chapter's focal ideas into action in their own middle or high school English classroom.
- *Key Takeaway Points.* Each of these chapters concludes with a list of key takeaway points and an infographic that displays major ideas from the chapter in a visually appealing format.

Chapter 8 of the book, "Implementing This Approach: Suggestions for Classroom Practice," shares important recommendations designed to help teachers incorporate inquiry-based grammar instruction in their classrooms. The information in this chapter synthesizes key points from the book, provides essential suggestions for utilizing the ideas described in the text, and includes sample lessons and steps that show how to put the book's ideas into action. The concluding chapter, "Why Inquiry- and Asset-Based Grammar Instruction Makes a Difference," provides closing insights that convey the importance of this approach to providing students with student-centered and meaningful grammar instruction that draws on the assets and experiences they bring to the classroom. The book also provides two appendices that can be useful to teachers as they incorporate asset-based grammar instruction into the classroom. Appendix A, "A Guide for Book Studies," provides discussion questions to prompt conversation for teachers engaging in a professional book study with this text. It provides questions for teachers to reflect on after reading each of the book's chapters. Finally, Appendix B, "Reproducible Charts and Forms to Use in Your Classroom," shares easy-to-use graphic organizers for teachers to use in their instruction as they implement inquiry-based grammar instruction in their classrooms.

The inquiry- and asset-based instructional practices described in this book can reshape grammar instruction in culturally sustaining and meaningful ways. I'm thrilled that you're exploring this important and innovative instructional approach. To take the next step towards learning more, keep reading!

1
Building the Foundation for Inquiry-Based and Asset-Focused Grammar Instruction

An essential aspect of successful inquiry-based and asset-focused grammar instruction is working with students to establish foundational knowledge and understanding that will help them succeed in this work. As we'll explore in this chapter, before students conduct their own grammar inquiries, it's essential that we teachers help them understand the features of the grammatical concepts they'll be exploring, the importance of those concepts, and the key components of the inquiries they'll be conducting.

This chapter is designed to give you the information you'll need to build the foundation for the inquiry-based grammar work described in this book. It begins by describing what establishing a foundation for this type of grammar instruction consists of, identifying important instructional objectives and corresponding practices associated with inquiry-based and asset-focused grammar work. Next, the chapter discusses why establishing this foundation—and the teaching and learning activities that are essential to building it—are important to students' successful experiences with grammar inquiries. After that, it explores how instructional practices that build the foundation for inquiry-based grammar instruction look in action, providing examples from my work with seventh- and tenth-grade English classes. Following those classroom connections, the chapter shares key instructional suggestions to keep in mind when establishing the foundation for your own students to engage in inquiry-based grammar instruction. At the end of the chapter, you'll find important takeaway points to consider and an infographic that displays that information. Now let's look closely at each of these ideas, which, when taken together, will help you develop a strong understanding of what it means to build a foundation for inquiry-based and asset-focused grammar instruction, why doing so is important, and how it can look in action.

What Is It?

The initial step of engaging in the inquiry-based and asset-focused grammar instruction described in this book is establishing a strong foundation in the grammar concepts students will study and the features of the inquiries in which the students will engage. To effectively build these foundations, I recommend focusing first on the grammatical concept on which students will focus in their inquiries and then introducing to students the components of the inquiries themselves. In this section, we'll first look at how to build students' fundamental knowledge of grammatical concepts; once they have this knowledge, they'll be able to conduct inquiries into authentic uses of those concepts. After we explore together how to develop that essential knowledge, we'll look at ways to introduce students to the grammar inquiries they'll be conducted; this will help students understand what they'll be doing and the benefits of this practice.

Build Fundamental Knowledge of Grammatical Concepts

Before students begin the process of looking at real-world examples of grammatical concepts and analyzing the significance of those concepts to real-world situations, they need to develop understandings of the elements of grammar that will be central to their inquiries. For example, if students are going to look at examples of subordinate clauses in authentic settings, they first need to understand what subordinate clauses are and why authors use them. To build these understandings, I recommend engaging students in three instructional steps, each of which is listed and described here:

1. Conduct an introductory mini-lesson on the focal grammatical concept.
   To introduce students to the essential features of the grammatical concept on which they'll be focusing throughout their inquiry experience, I like to begin with an introductory mini-lesson. The goal of this mini-lesson is to give students a first step into their work with the grammatical concept. When I teach these mini-lessons, I do three things: 1) I introduce key features of the concept, 2) I provide engaging and accessible examples, and 3) I write the features and examples on anchor charts and post them in the classroom for reference throughout the inquiry and later in the school year.

For example, in a mini-lesson on subordinate clauses, I begin with introductory information about what subordinate clauses are, identifying their fundamental features and how they're used in sentences. I then share with students some engaging examples of subordinate clauses I've created, incorporating information about popular culture and/or events taking place in the school. As I share these examples and explanations, I write them on chart paper; after class, I post that chart paper on the classroom wall. Throughout this discussion, I emphasize to students that this is just the first step of our work with that concept and that they're not expected to memorize this information. I share with the students that we'll be working with the focal concept and learning a lot about it and that this mini-lesson is the starting point.

2. Show students published examples of the concept.
After introducing students to the fundamental features of the grammatical concept on which they'll be focusing during their inquiries, I like to share with them published examples of that concept. When selecting these published examples, I find fiction and nonfiction books that I believe could engage my students and are accessible to them and then look through those books for examples of the focal concept. For example, when talking with tenth graders about subordinate clauses, I shared with them the following example from the book *The Hate U Give* by Angie Thomas (2017): "When my feet touch the cold floor, goose bumps pop all over me" (p. 31).

3. Talk with students about the importance of the concept to the published examples.
This step is designed to deepen students' understandings of the focal grammatical concepts: now that the students have seen published examples of those concepts, they can think further about them by discussing the importance of the concept to the published text they examined. This practice helps students reflect on why the author of the published piece used the grammatical concept they did and the way that the concept enhances the effectiveness of the text. For instance, after my students looked at the published subordinate clause example in the excerpt from *The Hate U Give* discussed in the preceding section ("When my feet touch the cold floor, goose bumps pop all over me" (Thomas, 2017, p. 31)), I talked with them about the importance of the subordinate clause "When my feet touch the cold floor" to the sentence. We discussed how the excerpt would still function as a complete sentence if it only contained the independent clause "goose bumps pop all over me," but it wouldn't have the

same level of detail and explanation as it does with the subordinate clause added. By talking with students about the importance of these grammatical concepts, we can help them deepen their understandings of how grammar is an important tool to effective communication. Students will draw on this knowledge as they engage in their grammar inquiries.

Introduce the Grammar Inquiries to Students

Once you've worked with students to build their fundamental knowledge of a specific grammatical concept, the next step is to introduce to them the work they'll do in their grammar inquiries. When I introduce these inquiries to students, I explain that they'll now be taking their knowledge of the grammatical concept they've been exploring into a new setting by looking for examples of that concept in their out-of-school lives. For example, when I explained to the tenth graders with whom I was working that they would be engaging in grammar inquiries related to subordinate clauses, I shared the assignment description depicted in Figure 1.1.

When sharing this information, I explain to students that they'll be working to identify and analyze examples of the focal concept in their out-of-school lives. While the specific grammatical concepts you'll analyze with students will vary as you and your students study different concepts, the principles of grammar inquiries, in which students consider essential questions focused on the importance of grammatical concepts to everyday communication, identify and analyze examples, and reflection on their experiences, remain consistent. In these explanations, I emphasize the following points to students:

- They will look for examples in their everyday lives of the grammatical concept we've been studying.
- Those examples can be found in a very wide range of texts!
- Once they identify the examples, they will analyze why the focal grammatical concept is important to the text in which it is used.
- I will support them in class while they work on these analyses.
- They will share the results of their inquiries by describing their identifications of the focal concept and their analyses of why the concept is significant to the text in which it appears.
- After completing the inquiry, they will reflect on what they learned from the experience.

This information provides students with clear understandings of the features of the inquiries in which they'll engage and prepares them to apply their knowledge of grammar in inquiry-based and asset-focused ways.

Subordinate Clause Grammar Inquiry Description

Great job on our recent work with subordinate clauses! In our recent conversation on this topic, you have learned about the features of subordinate clauses, looked at examples of them in published books, and thought about the importance of this concept to the published texts in which those examples appeared.

Now, we're going to take our work with subordinate clauses to the next level by engaging in grammar inquiries about this concept! In these inquiries, we're going to examine the essential question "Why are subordinate clauses important tools for communication in our everyday lives?" To conduct these inquiries, you'll look for examples of subordinate clauses in texts you encounter in your everyday lives, analyze the importance of those subordinate clauses to the texts in which they're used, and reflect on what you learned from the experience.

The everyday texts in which you identify subordinate clauses can take a very wide range of forms! Some possibilities are listed here, but this is not a complete list. I will work with you through the process, so please let me know if you have any questions!

Here are some possible texts in which you might identify subordinate clauses:

- Song lyrics
- Social media posts
- Online conversations
- Conversations with family, friends, and/or community members
- Articles about news and current events
- Movies and shows
- Sports broadcasts
- Your own creative writing
- Books you read outside of school

Figure 1.1 Subordinate Clause Grammar Inquiry Description

Why Is It Important?

Establishing a strong foundation for inquiry-based and asset-focused grammar instruction is essential to helping students have successful experiences with this approach to teaching and learning. Both of the key components of establishing this foundation—building fundamental knowledge of grammatical concepts and introducing the grammar inquiries to students—play important roles in students' successes with inquiry-based grammar instruction. In this section, we'll look together at why each of these foundational elements can help students be successful as they engage in grammar inquiries.

The Importance of Building Fundamental Knowledge of Grammatical Concepts

The process of building students' fundamental knowledge of grammatical concepts is essential to their work with grammar inquiries because of the way it helps students understand the features of the concepts they'll be studying, the ways those concepts appear when used in action, and the importance of those concepts to the texts in which they're used. The introductory minilesson on the focal grammatical concept begins to establish the foundational knowledge on which students will build throughout the inquiry process. The published mentor texts featuring the concept help students see that the focal concept is not just used in out-of-context examples, but also in authentic communication. Finally, discussions with students about the importance of the concept to the published mentor texts in which they appear introduce students to the practice of analyzing the significance of grammatical concepts to texts. Students will draw on all of these understandings and skills throughout their grammar inquiries.

The Importance of Introducing Grammar Inquiries to Students

In my experience, grammar inquiries are unlike any other work that students have done when learning about and analyzing grammatical concepts. Because of this, I feel it is essential to provide students with clear and detailed introductions to the concepts of grammar inquiries before they begin their work with this learning process. When we share with students the features of the grammar inquiries they'll conduct and the work they'll do in this experience, we are giving them clear expectations and concrete guidelines that will facilitate their success. For example, when I shared with my students the subordinate clause grammar inquiry assignment description in Figure 1.1 of this chapter and talked with them about them about the components of this inquiry, I explained the features of this project and the ways that it builds on the work they had done up to that point with grammar instruction. In this assignment description, I reminded students of their recent work with subordinate clauses and then stated "Now, we're going to take our work with subordinate clauses to the next level by engaging in grammar inquiries about this concept!" By relating back to students' previous work and providing them with clear descriptions and explanations of the grammar inquiries they will conduct, we can help our students feel confident as they engage in this new learning experience.

How Can It Look in Action?

In this section, I share examples of my work with seventh- and tenth-grade English classes, focusing specifically on the ways I worked with my students to build the foundation for the inquiry-based and asset-focused grammar instruction that they would do throughout the project. First, let's look at how I worked with a class of seventh graders to help them understand the concept of strong verbs.

As my seventh graders fill up the classroom, I can't help but share my excitement for the work we'll do that day. "I'm so excited to keep talking with you about strong verbs," I tell them. I point to a piece of chart paper posted on the wall. Last class, we made this chart together. We talked about how strong verbs are clear and specific versions of verbs that show exactly how an action was performed. We compared them to weaker verbs by discussing how 'said' is an example of a weaker verb because we don't know exactly how the action was done, while 'shouted' is a strong verb because it shows us how the action took place.

As I say this, I motion to these examples on the chart paper.

"Today," I continue, "we're going to go deeper into this concept by looking at how it appears in published writing." I pick up the book Omar Rising *by Aisha Saeed (2022), which the class read earlier in the school year, and turn to page seven of the text. I use the document camera to project the page to the front of the room and explain to the students, "on this page, there are two great examples of strong verbs that we'll look at together." I point to the text and continue, "This sentence reads 'I glance at my mother' (Saeed, 2022, p. 7). Here, author Aisha Saeed uses the strong verb 'glance' to show how the action was performed." Students nod and verbally indicate agreement, and I continue: If the author used a weaker verb like 'look' instead of 'glance,' we wouldn't know exactly how Omar, the narrator and protagonist of this book, looked at his mother. The strong verb 'glance' tells us the specific way he looked at her.*

"Now, we'll look at another example of a strong verb that Aisha Saeed uses on the same page of Omar Rising,*" I inform the students. I point to the sentence "Amal pokes her head around the door" (Saeed, 2022, p. 7) and read it out loud. Next, I explain, In this sentence, Saeed uses the strong verb "pokes." This is an example of a strong verb because it shows us exactly how Amal moved her head. A weaker verb*

replacement could be something like "moves," which is a much more general description and can be done in a variety of ways. Now, let's hear from you all. Why do you think this strong verb is important to the effectiveness of this sentence?

I ask. Students around the classroom raise their hands and share their insights. One comments "The strong verb is important because it shows what happened really clearly. We know what it means when it says she pokes her head. It's a really clear description."

"Great response," *I praise the student. Addressing the whole class, I say* "Good work today, everyone. In our next class, we'll think further about the importance of strong verbs to effective writing. This will help you prepare for the grammar inquiries we'll be doing soon!"

Now, let's take a look at how I introduced the subordinate clause grammar inquiries described in Figure 1.1 to a class of tenth graders.

"You've been doing such a great job with subordinate clauses," I greet the students in the tenth-grade English class I'm teaching. *You've thought about the features of this concept, such as how subordinate clauses provide background and context to the information in the independent clauses in sentences. You've also looked carefully at published subordinate clauses and reflected on the importance of those subordinate clauses to the texts in which they're used.*

I ask the students to recall key ideas about what they've noticed so far from our discussions about the features and importance of subordinate clauses.

"Now," I continue,

we're going to take the next step in our work with subordinate clauses: we're going to do something called a grammar inquiry. In this project, we're going to think about the question 'Why are subordinate clauses important tools for communication in our everyday lives?' To conduct these inquiries, you'll look for examples of subordinate clauses in texts you encounter in your everyday lives, analyze the importance of those subordinate clauses to the texts in which they're used, and reflect on what you learned from the experience

I give each student the Subordinate Clause Grammar Inquiry Description document depicted earlier in this chapter and read it out loud. After reading it aloud, I emphasized some key components of the inquiries for the students:

In this project, you'll look for subordinate clauses in texts that you encounter in your everyday lives. The description we read together lists some possible texts where you might find subordinate clauses, like song lyrics, social media posts, and conversations, but there are other examples too. After you find at least one example of a subordinate clause in your everyday life, you'll analyze the importance of that subordinate clause to the text where you found it. For example, maybe you find a really important subordinate clause in a

> *song lyric: you would analyze why that subordinate clause is so significant to the song lyric. You might talk about what information it provides, why that information is important, and how the audience's experience with the song would be different if that subordinate clause wasn't there.*

I ask students to take a few minutes and reflect on what they notice about the grammar inquiry descriptions. We discuss key ideas that stand to them, what interests them about the work, and what questions they have.

I then continue by providing some introductory information about the presentation students will give and the reflection they will write:

> *We'll talk about all of this information in more detail as we move through the inquiry project, but I want to give you a little bit of a preview of what you'll do with the example you identify and analyze. After we take some time together to work on and discuss your identifications of subordinate clauses in your everyday life and your analyses of their importance, everyone will give a presentation in which you share the results of your inquiries. Once you do that, I'll ask you to reflect on your grammar inquiry experience and what you learned from it. I am very excited to see your work throughout this project. I'll provide more details and suggestions as we keep working. I'm looking forward to supporting you as you do this work!*

Instructional Recommendations

In this section, I share and describe four key instructional recommendations to consider as you work with your students to build the foundation for inquiry-based and asset-focused grammar instruction. The recommendations discussed in this section are:

1. Use the introductory mini-lessons to build students' foundational knowledge without overwhelming them.
2. Use mentor texts to familiarize students with the uses and importance of grammatical concepts.
3. Explain to students that grammar inquiries are authentic applications of their grammatical insights.
4. Share with students that you will support them through their identifications and analyses.

Now, let's take a look at each of these recommendations in detail.

Recommendation One: Use the Introductory Mini-Lessons to Build Students' Foundational Knowledge Without Overwhelming Them

When conducting the introductory mini-lesson at the beginning of this instructional process, it's important to build their foundational knowledge of the grammatical concept on which they'll be focusing and to do this without overwhelming them with specific details that they'll be expected to memorize. These mini-lessons provide an initial look at the grammatical concept on which students will be focused throughout their inquiries. Because of this, their purpose is not for students to learn everything possible about the concept at one time, but to provide students with an accessible first step on which they'll continue to build throughout the process. For instance, when I conducted an introductory mini-lesson on strong verbs with my seventh-graders, I explained that they weren't expected to memorize everything about that concept immediately. I wrote definitions and examples on a piece of chart paper and shared that I was doing so in order for them to have a resource to which they could refer.

"I'm writing this information on strong verbs on this chart, which will be an anchor chart for you to continue to use throughout our work on this topic," I shared with them. "I don't expect you to memorize everything about strong verbs right now," I continued. "We're going to continue to learn about this concept as we keep working with it. This mini-lesson is our first step and this anchor chart is something we'll return to as we talk more about strong verbs." Later in that unit, a student shared with me that he appreciated the support provided by this initial mini-lesson and its corresponding anchor chart. "The anchor chart you made about strong verbs was really helpful," the student told me. "I looked back at it a lot while we did our strong verb inquiries. I liked that I could always look at it when I needed a reminder."

Recommendation Two: Use Mentor Texts to Familiarize Students with the Uses and Importance of Grammatical Concepts

My next recommendation for setting students up for success in their grammar inquiries is to use mentor texts (published examples of the grammatical concepts they'll be studying) to develop their familiarity with and understandings of these concepts. This suggestion follows from the work done in the first recommendation: once you've used foundational mini-lessons and corresponding examples to show students key components of grammatical concepts, the next step is to extend their learning by discussing how these concepts are used in practice. Using mentor texts is a great tactic for helping students think deeply about grammatical concepts because it creates opportunities for students to look closely at how and why expert writers use these concepts to make their works as effective as possible.

To use mentor texts in this way, I recommend first revisiting the anchor chart explanation and examples introduced in the previous mini-lesson and then explaining that the class will follow up this work by looking at how published authors use that same grammatical concept. Next, I suggest sharing examples from published works that you believe students will find interesting and accessible that use the focal concept. For example, earlier in this chapter I identified a subordinate clause from *The Hate U Give* by Angie Thomas (2017) and strong verbs from *Omar Rising* by Aisha Saeed (2022) that I showed students to help them see how these concepts are used in published works. One useful tactic for sharing these mentor texts with students is to display text using a document camera and project it to the front of the classroom. As you read the text to students and they follow along, you can identify the published example of the focal concept in the text. Next, I suggest leading students in a conversation about the importance of that concept to the effectiveness of the text. For example, after I showed my tenth-grade students a subordinate clause example in *The Hate U Give*, we discussed the importance of that concept to the text, focusing on the information the clause provides and how it helps the reader understand the context and background associated with what is taking place in the sentence.

To facilitate these conversations and analyses of mentor text, I recommend using the Mentor Text Analysis Graphic Organizer depicted in Figure 1.2 and also available in Appendix B. This graphic organizer contains space to identify the focal grammatical concept, the mentor text title, the excerpt from the text, and thoughts about why the focal concept is important to the effectiveness of the text. By completing this chart with students, you can help them consider and develop understandings of the importance of the grammatical concepts that they will use in their inquiries.

Recommendation Three: Explain to Students That Grammar Inquiries are Authentic Applications of Their Grammatical Insights

Now that students have explored the features of the focal grammatical concepts, ways they're used in mentor texts, and why they are important to those texts, it's time to introduce the grammar inquiries to the students. When introducing the grammar inquiry projects to students, I recommend explaining to them that this work is an opportunity to apply their grammatical insights in authentic ways that connect to their out-of-school lives. To do this, I suggest explaining to students that they have developed key understandings of the focal concept through the work they've done up to that point and are now well positioned to use their knowledge to think more deeply about the concept and how it's used in the world around them. After sharing this information, I recommend providing students with a grammar inquiry project description that aligns with the focal concept, such as the example depicted in Figure 1.1.

Focal Grammatical Concept	Mentor Text Title	Excerpt from the Text	Why the Focal Concept is Important to the Effectiveness of the Text

Figure 1.2 Mentor Text Analysis Graphic Organizer

When sharing the project description with students, I encourage you to emphasize the essential question featured in that document and explain that they will use that essential question as the starting point as they consider how the focal concept relates to their out-of-school lives. For example, the essential question in the subordinate clause inquiry description in Figure 1.1 is "Why are subordinate clauses important tools for communication in our everyday lives?" It can be useful to then provide students with some possible types of texts they might encounter in their everyday lives that could feature the focal concept. For example, most grammatical concepts can be found in texts such as song lyrics, social media posts, movies and shows, and conversations with family, friends, and community members. After sharing this information, I recommend explaining to students why this project can be beneficial to them both as learners and as individuals. For example, when introducing both of the units discussed in chapter to my seventh and tenth graders, respectively, I emphasized that looking at and analyzing examples of the grammatical concept they've been studying will help them understand that concept in detail and will help them think carefully about grammar in their out-of-school lives, not just in the classroom. "We don't just use strong verbs in school," I told my seventh graders. "We use them all the time in real-world situations to make our communication stronger. The authentic examples we'll look at in these inquiries will help us think about that."

Recommendation Four: Share with Students That You Will Support Them Through Their Identifications and Analyses

Once you introduce and explain grammar inquiries to students, I recommend communicating to them that you will support them through their identifications of grammatical concepts in their everyday lives and their analyses of these examples. Grammar instruction has traditionally focused on worksheets and out-of-context exercises (Weaver, 1998) and has lacked a student-centered focus (Ruday, 2020a). Because of this, while grammar instruction that focuses on students' lives and out-of-school uses can certainly engage students, it's also very likely that this instructional approach is quite different from what they've experienced before. By explaining to students that you will support them as they identify and analyze grammatical concepts they encounter in out-of-school settings, you can help them feel more comfortable as they think about the ways they engage with the topic in their everyday lives.

One way to communicate this message of support to students is to explain to them that you will confer with them throughout the unit to make sure that they are identifying examples of the concept and to help them analyze the concept's importance. When I talked with my seventh graders about the strong verb grammar inquiries they would be conducting, I told them We will have days scheduled in this unit when you'll bring in examples of strong verbs you've found in your everyday lives. We'll look at those examples together and I'll support you as you analyze the importance of those examples to the texts where you find them.

These initial explanations can help students feel confident as they begin this learning experience. (Specific steps and practices for providing students with this support are described in Chapter 4: Helping Students Identify and Analyze Authentic Examples of Grammatical Concepts.)

Key Takeaway Points

This section provides key takeaway points to consider as you do the important instructional work of building the foundation for inquiry-based and asset-focused grammar instruction with your students.

- The initial step of engaging in the inquiry-based and asset-focused grammar instruction described in this book establishes a strong foundation in the grammar concepts students will study and the features of the inquiries in which the students will engage.
- To establish this foundation, I recommend doing the following:
  - First, build students' fundamental knowledge of a grammatical concept by conducting an introductory mini-lesson on the topic, showing students published examples of the concept, and talking with them about the importance of the concept to the published examples.
  - Next, introduce the students to the work they'll do in their grammar inquiries by explaining that they'll be working to identify and analyze examples of the focal concept in their out-of-school lives.
- Both of these practices are very important to students' successes in grammar inquiries:
  - Building students' fundamental knowledge of grammatical concepts is essential to their work with grammar inquiries because of the way it helps students understand the features, applications, and importance of the concept they'll be studying.
  - Introducing the features of the grammar inquiries to students provides them with clear expectations and concrete guidelines that will facilitate their success, which is especially important because this instructional process may be unfamiliar or unique for students.
- When working with your students to build the foundation for inquiry-based and asset-focused grammar instruction, I recommend following these instructional recommendations:
  - Use the introductory mini-lessons to build students' foundational knowledge without overwhelming them.
  - Use mentor texts to familiarize students with the uses and importance of grammatical concepts.

- Explain to students that grammar inquiries are authentic applications of their grammatical insights.
- Share with students that you will support them through their identifications and analyses.
◆ The infographic in Figure 1.3 depicts these instructional recommendations.

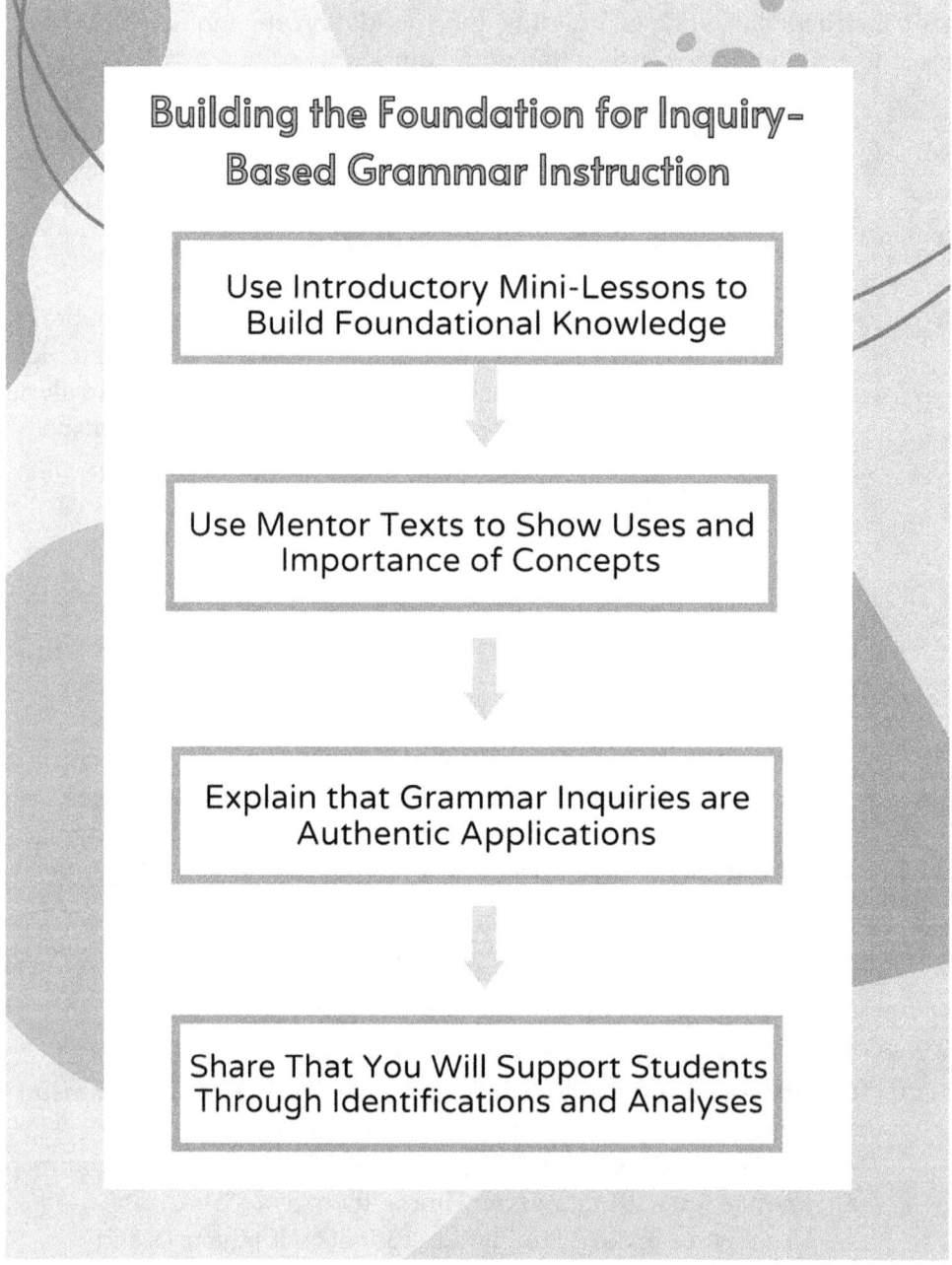

Figure 1.3 Infographic—Building the Foundation for Inquiry-Based Grammar Instruction

2
Showing Students Examples of Authentically Used Grammatical Concepts

After working with your students to build the foundation for inquiry-based and asset-focused grammar instruction, you and your students can move forward with thinking about how grammatical concepts are used in authentic, real-world situations. This chapter will prepare you to do just that. It focuses on the next step of the grammar inquiry instructional process: showing students examples of authentically used grammatical concepts. As we'll explore in this chapter, showing these examples to students gives them strong understandings of what it looks like to identify authentic, real-world examples of grammatical concepts they encounter in their out-of-school lives.

The chapter begins by explaining what it means to show authentically used examples of grammatical concepts, providing information about the essential aspects and features of doing so. After that, it discusses why this practice is especially important to students' experiences with inquiry-based grammar instruction before then sharing ways that it can look in action in the classroom. Following those explanations and examples, the chapter provides instructional recommendations to keep in mind when putting its key insights into action in your classroom and concludes with some closing takeaway points and a useful infographic. Now, let's begin our exploration of this important component of inquiry-based and asset-focused grammar instruction!

DOI: 10.4324/9781003424260-3

What Is It?

In this step of the grammar inquiry process, we model for our students what it looks like to identify examples of grammatical concepts we encounter in our everyday, out-of-school lives.

We can do this by identifying the grammatical concept on which students will focus on in their own inquiries and sharing one or more examples of that concept from our own lives. These concepts can be found in any kind of text at all, including but not limited to television shows, movies, song lyrics, verbal conversations, emails, text messages, social media posts, news articles, books we read for enjoyment, and many other possibilities. Figure 2.1 lists these and some other possible texts in which we can find grammatical concepts in our everyday lives that we might share with students.

Since grammatical concepts are applicable not just to school but also to real-world, authentic contexts, we can show our students examples of these concepts in our out-of-school lives from a wide range of texts and situations. For instance, I recently spoke with a middle-school English class about the concept of prepositional phrases. Before asking them to find prepositional phrases in their own lives, I talked with them about a variety of examples of prepositional phrases I had recently encountered in my everyday life. To describe one such situation, I shared this anecdote about the prepositional phrases I used when talking to a visitor to my town: "Someone was visiting the town where I live and I gave them directions to a place they were trying to find. I noticed that I frequently used prepositional phrases when giving those directions. I used the prepositional phrases 'on the highway,' 'past the shopping center,' and 'across the road' when telling them how to get to the place they wanted to find." This is just one example of a grammatical concept used

Texts Where We Can Find Grammatical Concepts in our Everyday Lives
• Television shows
• Movies
• Song lyrics
• Podcasts
• Sports broadcasts
• Text messages
• Emails
• Verbal conversations
• Verbal stories we tell each other
• News articles and broadcasts
• Books we read for enjoyment
• Our own creative writing and journaling

Figure 2.1 Some Texts Where We Can Find Grammatical Concepts in Our Everyday Lives

in an out-of-school, real-world situation. When working with students on a particular grammatical concept, you'll identify examples of that concept that you encounter in authentic situations and share that information with students. A wonderful aspect of this activity is that there are so many situations and examples we might use since grammatical tools are used in a wide range of texts, providing us with a plethora of opportunities to find and incorporate these authentic examples. In the next section, we'll look together at why this practice is important to inquiry-based grammar instruction.

Why Is It Important?

When we show our students examples of the grammatical concepts they'll explore in their inquiries that we've identified in our own authentic communication, we incorporate an instructional practice that is beneficial to our students in a number of ways. Two key reasons that this practice is important are that it provides a model for what students will be asked to do in their own grammar inquiries and it emphasizes that grammatical concepts are important in all communication contexts, not just those addressed in grammar textbooks and exercises. Now, let's take a look at each of these benefits and discuss their importance.

It Provides a Model for Students

When we show our students examples of grammatical concepts that we encounter in our everyday lives, we model for them the kind of work that they'll do in their own grammar inquiries. Since, as discussed in Chapter 1, grammar inquiries are unlike most methods of grammar instruction and are likely new experiences for students, our students can greatly benefit from seeing what the steps of the inquiry look like before embarking on their own. By modeling for students what it looks like to find authentic, real-world examples of a grammatical concept, we provide them with clear expectations and guidelines that will support them when they do this work on their own. By giving students a clear target to attain in their work, we create an environment that maximizes their confidence. Without this model and corresponding clear expectations, our students may not feel as comfortable engaging in this work. At the conclusion of the grammar inquiries on strong verbs that my seventh graders conducted, one student shared that he benefited from the examples I shared from my out-of-school communication: "I liked that you showed us examples from strong verbs from your life before we found some from ours. That helped me know what to do and how to do it."

It Emphasizes the Importance of Grammatical Concepts to All Communication

Another key benefit of this instructional practice is that it emphasizes the significant role that grammatical concepts play in all communication contexts and texts, not just those in textbooks and grammar exercises. A key principle behind the grammar inquiries that students conduct is that grammatical concepts are essential tools for communication and are used in a wide range of situations that we all encounter in our everyday lives, including but not limited to the texts identified in Figure 2.1. By highlighting the role of these concepts in authentic settings, we can make our grammar instruction as culturally relevant (Ladson-Billings, 1995) and culturally sustaining (Paris, 2012); these real-world applications of grammar can center students' identities and experiences in ways that out-of-context grammar instruction does not. When we as teachers share examples of grammatical concepts from our authentic communication, we convey to our students that grammar is a tool used in a variety of situations, which helps create a classroom in which real-world connections and applications are recognized and valued.

How Can It Look in Action?

This section provides examples of how I showed authentically used grammatical concepts with students in seventh- and tenth-grade English classes. In these instructional snapshots, you'll find descriptions of important components of these discussions. We'll first take a look at how I shared this information to my seventh graders.

I begin today's seventh-grade English class by directing students to the text projected to the front of the room, "Strong Verbs in the Real World," and then talk with them about this information: "Today, we'll be talking about examples of strong verbs in the real world. As you know, we've been talking recently about our grammar inquiries, which will be on the importance of strong verbs to communication in your everyday life. Before you look for those examples of strong verbs in your everyday lives and analyze their importance, I want to share with you some examples of strong verbs I've noticed in my everyday life. I'm showing you these examples so that you have a good understanding of what kinds of things to look for when you do this on your own."

"You all know that I'm a sports fan and that I love the Pittsburgh Steelers," I continue smiling. "I'm going to show you some examples of strong verbs from a recent conversation I had with one of my children about a Steelers game. First, let's take a look at this example." I change the slide projected to the front of the room to one that reads "Najee Harris sprinted past the defense!" Next, I begin to talk with my students about the text on the slide: "When I was talking with one of my sons about

a Steelers game, he described a play in which a player named Najee Harris scored a touchdown. In this description, he said the information you see on this slide: 'Najee Harris sprinted past the defense!' When doing so, he used the strong verb 'sprinted' when describing what the player did. This is a great example of a strong verb because it describes exactly how Najee Harris went past the defense. Like we recently discussed, strong verbs are specific and clear action words that show exactly how something was done. 'Sprinted' is a strong verb that provides this information."

Next, I move to a new slide that reads "The players rushed onto the field to join the celebration." I explained to my students, "This is a sentence from the same conversation I had with one of my kids about a Steelers game. In this sentence, my son described what took place at the end of the game and used a strong verb while doing so. Does anyone see an example of a strong verb here?" I call on a student who identifies "rushed" as a strong verb example. "Great job identifying this," I say. "'Rushed' is definitely a strong verb here. Why is this an example of a strong verb?"

The same student replies "'It's a strong verb because it tells you the way they went onto the field. You can tell how they did it."

"Absolutely right," I respond. "'Rushed' is a strong verb because it shows exactly how this action was performed."

Now let's take a look at how I showed tenth-grade students authentically used examples of subordinate clauses.

I open tenth-grade English today's class by reminding them of our previous discussion of their grammar inquiries and then explaining that I'll be modeling the kinds of real-world connections to grammatical concepts that they'll do in those inquiries: "In our last class, we discussed the grammar inquiries that you'll be conducting on subordinate clauses. We talked about how, in this project, you'll look for examples of subordinate clauses in texts that you'll encounter in your everyday life, and we talked about the wide range of texts where you might find these, like song lyrics, social media posts, conversations, movies, shows, and others. Today, I'm going to talk with you about some examples of subordinate clauses I recently encountered in my everyday life. This can give you an example of what a grammar inquiry can look like."

"The examples I'm going to share are both from a discussion I had with a friend about a ten-mile race that he's going to run," I told my students. "I ran this race before, and he asked about any recommendations I had for running the race, especially since it's really hilly. When I was talking with him about the race, I used a lot of subordinate clauses. One of the subordinate clauses I used was in the sentence on this slide." I project a slide that reads "Since the first two miles are all uphill, I suggest starting the race at an easy pace." I point to the slide, read the text out loud, and tell the students, "In this statement, I used the subordinate clause 'Since the first two miles are all uphill.' This part of the sentence is a subordinate clause because it begins with a subordinating conjunction–in this case, the word 'since'—and it gives background and context about the independent clause in the sentence. We've talked before about how subordinate clauses start with subordinating conjunctions and give

us information that help us understand the independent clause. In this sentence, the subordinate clause 'since the first two miles are all uphill' does these things."

I then move to a new slide that reads "I love the middle part of the race because there is a big, cheering crowd there." I tell my students, "This sentence is from the same conversation I had with my friend about the ten-mile race. I also used a subordinate clause in this sentence to explain my thoughts on the race. Where do you think the subordinate clause is in this sentence?"

The student I call on states "'Because there is a big, cheering crowd there' is a subordinate clause."

"Great job," I reply. "Why do you think it's a subordinate clause?"

"It's one," the student explains, "because it begins with a subordinating conjunction and it gives extra information about the independent clause."

"Wonderful work," I praise the student's response. "In this sentence, 'I love the middle part of the race' is the independent clause. Just as you said, the subordinate clause 'because there is a big, cheering crowd there' starts with the subordinating conjunction 'because' and provides important background and context that helps us understand the independent clause in more detail. We'll keep working on our inquiries related to subordinate clauses next class. Great job today!"

Instructional Recommendations

Now, we'll look together at four instructional recommendations to keep in mind as you share examples of authentically used grammatical concepts with your students. These recommendations, which will help you make this important activity as beneficial to your students as possible, are as follows:

1. Explain to students that you're modeling the work they'll do in their grammar inquiries.
2. Highlight the wide range of texts in which grammatical concepts are used.
3. Use your examples as a way to build a classroom community.
4. Help students understand the features of the examples you share.

Let's examine each of these recommendations individually, exploring how and why to put each one into practice in the classroom.

Recommendation One: Explain to Students That You're Modeling the Work They'll Do in Their Grammar Inquiries

Before sharing with students authentic examples of grammatical concepts that you've identified in your own life, I recommend explaining to students that this is a model of the work they'll do in their own inquiries. Doing so provides meaningful context to the work and clearly communicates to students the importance of the activity. When sharing these explanations with students, I suggest doing three things: 1) Remind students of the focus of their own grammar inquiries, 2) Tell them that you'll be sharing real-world examples from your own life of the concept they're studying, and 3) Explain that you're doing this to help students understand what to do in their own inquiries. By incorporating these three components into your initial explanation of the activity, you'll help students understand why this activity is important to their successful grammar inquiry work.

For example, in the classroom teaching description earlier in this chapter that describes how I shared authentic examples of strong verbs from my everyday life with my seventh graders, I connected the activity with the work they'll do in their own projects by saying "Before you look for those examples of strong verbs in your everyday lives and analyze their importance, I want to share with you some examples of strong verbs I've noticed in my everyday life. I'm showing you these examples so that you have a good understanding of what kinds of things to look for when you do this on your own." Similarly, when sharing real-world examples of subordinate clauses with tenth graders, I first reminded students of what they'll be doing in their grammar inquiries and then explained "Today, I'm going to talk with you about some examples of subordinate clauses I recently encountered in my everyday life. This can give you an example of what a grammar inquiry can look like." In each of these discussions, I reminded students of the focus of their inquiries, communicated that I would be sharing my own real-world examples, and explained that this would help students in their own work. By establishing this context and purpose at the beginning of the activity, you'll let students know why you're sharing this information and how it can help them in their inquiry projects.

Recommendation Two: Highlight the Wide Range of Texts in Which Grammatical Concepts are Used

When talking with your students about authentic examples of grammatical concepts, I recommend emphasizing the wide range of real-world texts in which these elements of grammar are used. Highlighting the many everyday situations and texts that feature grammatical concepts can help students think differently about the importance and uses of grammar while also making their grammar inquiry projects feel more accessible and engaging. For instance, when we as teachers call attention to the many authentic and real-world forms of communication in which grammatical concepts are used, we can help our students see grammar as something with real-world relevance, rather than being an abstract series of rules with no connection to their authentic experiences. To help students understand the wide range of texts in which grammatical concepts appear, I recommend using the information in Figure 2.1, depicted earlier in this chapter. This figure illustrates the many authentic situations and contexts in which grammatical concepts are regularly used, such as text messages, television shows, song lyrics, and conversations.

When I share these authentic situations with students, I call attention to the idea that grammatical concepts can be found in any real-world communication context and that these are some examples of those forms of communication. When talking with the tenth-graders discussed in this chapter about subordinate clauses, I explained "Subordinate clauses are really important tools for communication, which is why you'll find them in so many different types of texts." I continued to emphasize that this concept, like all other grammatical concepts, go beyond the boundaries of the school: "We learn about grammar in school, but really these grammatical tools, like subordinate clauses and all other grammatical tools, go way beyond school. They are important to all kinds of communication in our everyday lives, from when we talk with our friends to when we listen to music to when we watch a show or movie." I concluded this explanation by relating the omnipresent nature of grammatical concepts to inquiry-based grammar instruction: "The grammar inquiries we're doing will help us see all of the ways grammar exists in real-world situations."

Recommendation Three: Use Your Examples as a Way to Build a Classroom Community

When we model our own identifications of grammatical concepts from our authentic communications and out-of-school lives, we can show our students aspects of our own interests and identities. For instance, in the examples that I shared with students described earlier in this chapter, I conveyed my interests in the Pittsburgh Steelers and in running. Since grammar inquiries are based on authentic situations and the uses of grammatical concepts in those contexts, they provide great opportunities for us as teachers to share aspects of our own identities and interests that we would like to make known to our students. In addition to making grammar instruction meaningful and engaging, the practice of sharing authentic examples of concepts we use and/or encounter in our out-of-school lives can also help build a classroom community. When we share aspects of our real-world interests with our students, we share components of our authentic selves, which helps our students learn about us and see us as individuals (Cushman, 2003). This practice contributes toward building a classroom environment in which our students trust us and see meaningful parts of who we are (Cushman, 2003).

To use your grammar inquiries to help build a classroom community, I recommend first reflecting on aspects of your interests and identity that you would like to share with students. Once you've done that, I suggest thinking about texts that relate those aspects and contain examples of the grammatical concept on which you and your students are focusing. When sharing with my students the examples described in this chapter, I identified my interests in the Pittsburgh Steelers and in running as key components of my identity that I wanted to share and then reflected on texts from my everyday life that related to those topics and contained examples of our focal concepts. Sharing these examples, I felt, helped my students see me in an authentic way and helped construct a classroom environment in which individuals' interests are celebrated. One student in the seventh-grade class shared with me that he enjoyed hearing about my interest in the Steelers while providing examples of strong verbs: "I liked that you showed us that you love the Steelers and that you talk about them with your son. I think that helped the class all know you better."

Recommendation Four: Help Students Understand the Features of the Examples You Share

Finally, when you share with your students authentic examples of grammatical concepts from your life, I recommend being strategic and purposeful as you help them understand the features of those examples. To do this, I suggest taking three related instructional steps, which combine to help students understand why an example represents a particular concept: 1) Share with students an authentic example of a grammatical concept, 2) Think aloud about why the example represents the concept it does, 3) Show the students another example of a grammatical concept, 4) Ask them to explain why it is an example of that concept. I used this approach in the instructional descriptions featured in the "How It Can Look in Action Section" earlier in this chapter. When talking about strong verbs with my seventh graders and subordinate clauses with my tenth graders, I showed an example of the focal grammatical concept, thought aloud about its features, showed them a new example of the concept, and then asked students to explain why that example represented that concept.

To plan for this instruction and support your students as you help them understand the features of the examples you share, I recommend using the graphic organizer depicted in Figure 2.2 (and also available in Appendix B). This graphic organizer contains designated spaces for you to identify a first authentic example of a grammatical concept you'll share with students, record your thoughts about how you'll think-aloud about its features, provide another example of the grammatical concept, and list your students' insights regarding why it exemplifies the concept.

I recommend completing the first three parts of the graphic organizer before class, sharing the information from those sections with students in the class discussion, and then completing the final component of the graphic

Authentic Example of Focal Grammatical Concept	Think-Aloud Points About its Features You'll Share with Students	Another Example of the Grammatical Concept	Students' Insights Regardings its Features

Figure 2.2 Graphic Organizer: Examples and Features of Grammatical Concepts

organizer during class as students share their responses. I like to project the graphic organizer using a document camera and write down the students' insights in the final section as they share them—I feel that this validates students' work by showing them that the teacher is recording their insights and ideas.

Key Takeaway Points

This section features key takeaway points to consider as you show students authentically used examples of grammatical concepts, a practice that will help students as they engage in their own grammar inquiries.

- In this step of the grammar inquiry process, we model for our students what it looks like to find examples of grammatical concepts in our everyday, out-of-school lives.
- We can do this by identifying the grammatical concept on which students will focus on in their own inquiries and sharing one or more examples of that concept from our own authentic experiences,
- Since grammatical tools are used in a wide range of texts and in so many situations, there are many opportunities to find these authentic examples, such as conversations, songs, movies, shows, and many other forms of communication. Figure 2.1 in this chapter lists some possible texts in which we can find grammatical concepts in our everyday lives that we might share with students.
- There are two key reasons why this practice is particularly important:
  - It provides a model for what students will be asked to do in their own grammar inquiries.
  - It emphasizes that grammatical concepts are important in all communication contexts, not just those addressed in grammar textbooks and exercises.
- When sharing examples of authentically used grammatical concepts with your students, I recommend using these instructional ideas:
  - Explain to students that you're modeling the work they'll do in their grammar inquiries.
  - Highlight the wide range of texts in which grammatical concepts are used.
  - Use your examples as a way to build a classroom community.
  - Help students understand the features of the examples you share.
- The infographic in Figure 2.3 depicts these instructional recommendations.

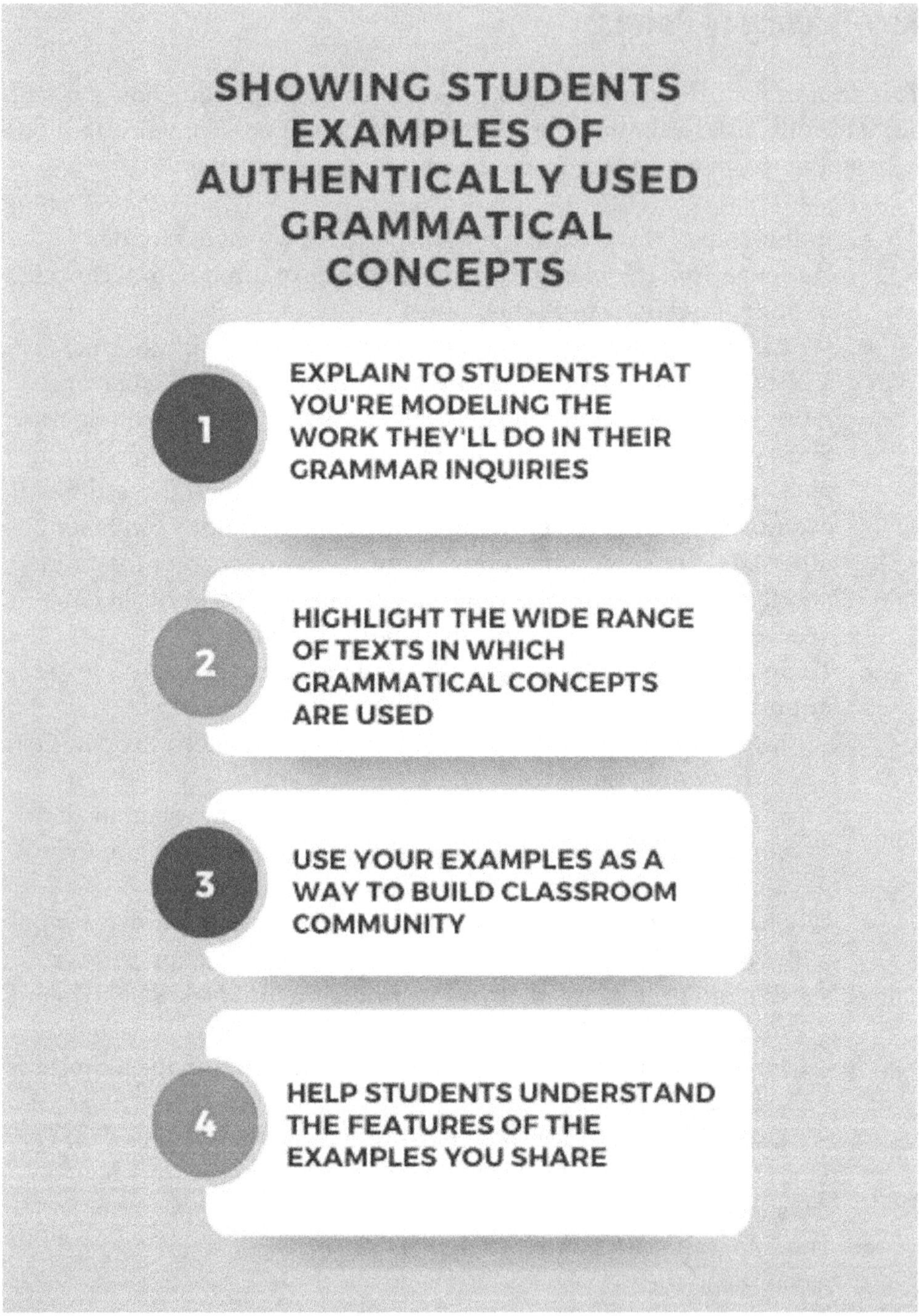

SHOWING STUDENTS EXAMPLES OF AUTHENTICALLY USED GRAMMATICAL CONCEPTS

1. EXPLAIN TO STUDENTS THAT YOU'RE MODELING THE WORK THEY'LL DO IN THEIR GRAMMAR INQUIRIES

2. HIGHLIGHT THE WIDE RANGE OF TEXTS IN WHICH GRAMMATICAL CONCEPTS ARE USED

3. USE YOUR EXAMPLES AS A WAY TO BUILD CLASSROOM COMMUNITY

4. HELP STUDENTS UNDERSTAND THE FEATURES OF THE EXAMPLES YOU SHARE

Figure 2.3 Infographic—Showing Students Examples of Authentically Used Grammatical Concepts

3

Reflecting with Students on the Importance of Authentically Used Grammatical Concepts

Now that you've shown students examples of authentically used grammatical concepts, you and your students can work together to reflect on the importance of those concepts to the text in which they're used. In this next step of the grammar inquiry process, you'll support and talk with your students as they begin to think about the importance of grammatical concepts that are used in authentic, real-world situations. The explanations, examples, and ideas in this chapter will prepare you to reflect with your students on the importance of the grammatical concepts and the corresponding texts that you shared with them in the instructional activities described in Chapter 2, when you showed students examples of grammatical concepts used in authentic situations.

This chapter opens with information about what it means to reflect with students on the importance of authentically used grammatical concepts, identifying and discussing key components of this practice. Next, the chapter describes why this practice is important to inquiry-based and asset-focused grammar instruction, highlighting how it can facilitate students' understandings of the significance of authentically used grammatical concepts and prepare them to do similar analyses in their own inquiries. After that, it shares instructional examples of how this practice can look in the classroom by spotlighting my work with seventh- and tenth-grade English classes. The chapter then provides recommendations to keep in mind when incorporating its ideas in your teaching practices before closing with takeaway points and infographic that highlights key ideas. Let's get started on learning about this important part of inquiry-based grammar instruction!

DOI: 10.4324/9781003424260-4

What Is It?

This component of the grammar inquiry process builds on the instructional practices presented in Chapter 2, which focused on showing students authentically used grammatical concepts. After you've shown students those examples and helped them understand their features, you and your students can move to reflecting on the importance of those concepts to the texts in which they're used. There are two key aspects to these reflective discussions: 1) Discuss with students why the creator of the text may have used the concept, and 2) Discuss with students how the text would be different if the concept was not used. In this section, we'll explore both of these discussion components, explaining what it means to engage students in each one.

Discuss with Students Why the Creator of the Text May Have Used the Concept

A key component of reflecting with students on the importance of an authentically used grammatical concept is to talk with students about why the creator of the text that you've shared and discussed with them may have used the grammatical concept on which you're focusing. For instance, if you've shown students examples of specific noun use in a social media post, you can then engage them in a discussion of why the author of that post used the specific noun and the ways that using that concept impacted the effectiveness of the text. I recently shared such an example with middle-school students by showing them a social media post I wrote after visiting a city and remarking on the skyscrapers in its skyline. I posted a picture of the Pittsburgh skyline on Instagram and wrote "These skyscrapers are gorgeous against the summer sunset."

After sharing this example with students and identifying the specific noun "skyscrapers," I led students in a conversation about why I may have used that specific noun. During this discussion, I talked with the students about my reasons for using the term "skyscrapers," explaining to them, I used this specific noun because it expresses exactly what I'm talking about. It helps me communicate what I think is so gorgeous. By using the specific noun "skyscrapers," I can be sure that anyone who sees this post knows just what I'm referring to in my statement.

You can lead this type of discussion with your students when talking about any grammatical concepts in any kind of authentic, real-world text; it can be a text that you created, like the example I shared in this description, or any other one that you've identified. When leading these discussions, I like to emphasize the importance of the concept to the work in which it was used and the way using it helped the author express their intended message.

Discuss with Students How the Text would be Different if the Concept was Not Used

After you've talked with students about why a text's creator may have used a grammatical concept and emphasized the importance of that concept, I suggest following that conversation up with a discussion of how the text would be different if the focal grammatical concept was not used. These conversations allow students to further understand the impact of the grammar element being discussed through an opportunity to compare how the text looks with the focal concept with how it appears without that concept. For example, when conducting this kind of discussion with the previously described Instagram post "These skyscrapers are gorgeous against the summer sunset," I compared the original text with a revised version that did not contain the specific noun "skyscrapers." In the revised text, I replaced "skyscrapers" with "buildings," which is a vaguer and more general noun. I placed both sentences next to each other on a slide and talked with students about how different the sentence was without the specific noun, asking them for their thoughts on how their experience reading the revised sentence was different from their experience reading the original one.

When conducting these discussions with your students, I recommend following a similar instructional process. Specifically, I suggest replacing or removing the focal grammatical concept from the original text, displaying both versions on a slide so that students can see both at the same time, and talking with students about how the two versions are different. During these discussions, I like to ask students to compare their experiences reading both texts—this can facilitate their analysis of the importance of the concept to the way they make sense of and understand the text, which ultimately leads to their awareness of the significance of the focal grammatical concept. There are a variety of grammatical concepts that you can identify and discuss in this activity—some, like punctuation and capitalization, are used primarily for clarity, while others, like prepositional phrases and relative clauses, involve details that the creator of a piece adds. No matter the specific grammatical concept, discussing with students how the sentence would look with that grammatical concept removed or replaced can help them think about the significance of that concept to the text in which it is used. Now, let's look at why this instructional practice is important to inquiry-based grammar instruction.

Why Is It Important?

Reflecting with students on the significance of authentically used grammatical concepts that we've shared and discussed with them is very important to students' experiences with inquiry-based grammar instruction. In this section, we'll look together at two key reasons why this instructional practice is so significant: 1) It shows students the kind of analysis they will conduct in their own grammar inquiries and 2) It develops the analytical skills that students will apply to their own inquiries. Let's examine each of the ideas and consider their importance to students' experiences with inquiry-based grammar instruction.

It Shows Students the Kind of Analysis They Will Conduct in Their Own Grammar Inquiries

When we talk with students about the significance of the authentically used grammatical concepts that we've shared with them, we provide them with a model for the kind of analysis they will conduct in their own grammar inquiries. By participating in these discussions regarding the importance of authentic grammatical concepts to the texts in which they are used, students will develop clear understandings of what it looks like to analyze the significance of a grammatical concept used in a real-world text. For example, if you talk with your students about the importance of a specific noun in a text that you encounter in your everyday life and engage them in an in-depth discussion that focuses on its significance to the text in which it was used, your students will be able to apply the same thought process to their own analyses of examples they identify in their own inquiries. If, for instance, you and your students discuss why the creator of a text may have used a certain grammatical concept and how the text would be different if that concept was not used, students will gain familiarity and comfort with these analytical activities. When students engage in their own inquiries, they can draw on these experiences and their familiarity with them as they conduct their own analyses.

It Develops the Analytical Skills that Students Will Apply to Their Own Inquiries

When students participate in discussions about the importance of authentically used grammatical concepts that you've identified to the texts in which they appear, they learn more than just how to analyze that particular example: they also develop the ability to analyze the significance of other grammatical concepts used in real-world situations, which prepares them to engage in their own grammar inquiries. The analytical abilities that students develop in these discussions are transferable skills that they can apply to other analyses they conduct, such as the work they do in their grammar inquiries. For example, a student who participates in a discussion about a specific noun that you've identified in your out-of-school doesn't just learn how to analyze that example: they also learn how to analyze all of the other examples of authentically used grammatical concepts that they encounter. Students who develop the abilities to analyze and understand the importance of authentically used grammatical concepts that you share with them foster the ability to conduct these same analyses of other examples they'll encounter, which will serve them well in their grammar inquiries.

How Can It Look in Action?

I share here instructional examples of how I worked with seventh- and tenth-grade English classes on the topic of reflecting on the importance of authentically used grammatical concepts. These classroom snapshots contain descriptions of key aspects of these learning activities. First, we'll look together at how I worked with my seventh graders to help them think about the importance of an authentically used grammatical concept.

As my seventh-graders enter the classroom, they see a slide in the front of the room that reads: "Strong Verbs in the Real World: Why are They Important?" Students quickly take their seats and examine the text on the slide. As they do so, I provide context for the information they're reading: "In our last class," I remind them,

> we looked at examples of strong verbs in real-world situations. I showed you two examples of strong verbs from a recent conversation I had with one of my children about a Pittsburgh Steelers game. Today, we're going to think further about those examples: since we identified them in our last conversation, we're going to talk today about why those strong verb examples are so important.

"To get started," I continue, "take a look at the first example of an authentically used grammatical concept that we talked about last time." I advance to the next slide, which contains the text "Najee Harris sprinted past the defense!" I direct the students' attention to the text and comment further on it:

> In our last class, we looked at this example and discussed the fact that 'sprinted' is a strong verb because it's a specific and clear action word that shows exactly how the action was performed. Today, we're going to think together about the importance of this strong verb to the conversation in which it was used. To do this, we're going to talk about two related topics: first, why we think my son may have used this strong verb in the conversation and, second, how this statement would be different if he didn't use that strong verb.

I move to a new slide; this one contains the same text—"Najee Harris sprinted past the defense!"—as well as the discussion question "Why did my son use the strong verb 'sprinted' in this conversation?" I point out the discussion question on the new slide and ask students to reflect on it. "Take two minutes and write in your notebooks your thoughts on this question," I tell the students. "When writing on this topic, you might think about why he felt using this strong verb might make the sentence better and more effective. Then, share your response with a partner. After that, we'll ask for volunteers to share their ideas with the rest of the class." The students write their ideas and share with partners while I circulate and listen to their insights. I then ask for volunteers to share their ideas with the rest of the class. One student explains "I think he used the strong verb to help you picture what happened. When he says sprinted, he helps you understand the way the player went past the defense. Because he used that word, you can understand really well what happened."

"That's an outstanding response!" I praise the student. In your response, you do such a great job of reflecting on the importance of the strong verb 'sprinted' and of using that knowledge to share your insights about why my son may have used it in his statement. You're absolutely right: the strong verb 'sprinted' shows us exactly how Najee Harris moved when he went past the defense. It creates a clear and vivid picture in the listener's mind and ensures that the listener understands what happened in the way that the speaker intended it. This strong verb makes sure that we know what took place and helps us visualize the action. It shows us that he wasn't jogging, walking, or anything else: he was sprinting. I heard other similar statements from other people in our class while I was circulating and listening to your insights. Great work!

"Now," I continue, "let's think about the second discussion topic: how this statement would be different if my son didn't use that strong verb." I advance to a new slide that contains the original statement—"Najee Harris sprinted past the defense!"—and a new discussion question: "How would the statement be different if my son didn't use that strong verb?" "In this question," I explain, "I'm asking you to think about how the information in the sentence would be different if that strong verb wasn't used. To help you think about this, I'm going to show you another slide: this one compares the original statement with a revised version that uses a weaker verb instead." I move to a slide that contains two statements: "Najee Harris sprinted past the defense!" and "Najee Harris went past the defense!"

I read the text of both sentences out loud and then tell the students their next directions: "Now that you've looked at both of these examples, please take two minutes to write how you think the sentence without the strong verb is different from the one with the strong verb. In other words, how do you think using 'went' instead of 'sprinted' changes the sentence? Please take two minutes to write a brief response and tell it to a partner. After that, I'll ask for volunteers to share their responses with the whole class."

I again circulate around the classroom and listen to students' responses as they talk with their partners. After doing so, I call the class together: "Great job sharing those ideas with your partners. Who would like to tell the rest of us your response?"
One student explains:

I think that the sentence without the strong verb is different because it's not specific like the sentence with the strong verb is. 'Went' isn't specific because it doesn't tell exactly how the football player did what he did. 'Sprinted' is specific because it does show us exactly how he did what he did.

"Excellent job!," *I exclaim.*

I love the way that you commented on how the strong verb provides specific information and shows us exactly how the action was performed. I also love how well you compared that version to the one with the weak verb, which. as you explained, does not tell us exactly how the action was performed. The word 'sprinted' definitely gives the specific detail to let us know how Najee Harris performed this action!

Next, the students engage in the same analytical and reflective work with the second strong verb I shared with them in the previous class—the verb "rushed" *in the sentence* "The players rushed onto the field to join the celebration." *After the students consider and comment on why my son used that strong verb and how the sentence would be different if a weaker verb was used, I praise their outstanding insights and thoughtful reflections:* "I'm so impressed by your great work today," *I tell them.* "You've done a wonderful job of thinking carefully about the importance of the strong verbs to these examples I've shown you. Fantastic work!"

Now, let's take a look at how I worked with tenth-graders as they analyzed the importance of authentically used subordinate clauses.

"Today," *I enthusiastically share with the students in a tenth-grade English class,* "we're going to take our work with subordinate clauses to the next level." *I motion to a slide projected at the front of the room that reads* "The Importance of Authentically Used Subordinate Clauses" *and then continue:*

We'll take our work to the next level by talking about the importance of authentically used subordinate clauses. We're going to look again at the subordinate clauses I showed you in our last class from a conversation I had with a friend about a ten mile race. One of these subordinate clauses was 'Since the first two miles are all uphill' in the sentence 'Since the first two miles are all uphill, I suggest starting the race at an easy pace.'

I advance to a slide that contains this sentence and direct students' attention to it. "First," I tell the students, "I'm going to ask you to think about why I used the subordinate clause in the sentence." I change the slide to a new one; this one contains the sentence "Since the first two miles are all uphill, I suggest starting the race at an easy pace" as well as the question "Why do you think I chose to use the subordinate clause 'Since the first two miles are all uphill?'" I read the text on the slide and then ask students to reflect on this question: "Write a brief response to this question," I tell them.

> *In this response, I want you to think about what kind of information this subordinate clause provides and what benefit might have come from my using it in this sentence. Thinking about these things will help you reflect on why I might have chosen to use it. After you write this reflection, share what you wrote with a partner. Then, we'll ask for volunteers to share your ideas with the rest of the class.*

I move around the classroom, listening to students' partner conversations, before asking for volunteers to share their thoughts. After students have shared their insights with partners, I ask for volunteers to share with the class. A student raises a hand and offers an explanation: "I think you chose to use it because it basically tells why you said what you did. It tells why you suggest starting the race at an easy pace. It's because the first two miles are uphill."
"Wonderful work sharing that insightful analysis!" I reply, praising the student.

> *The analysis and explanation you've provided is so thoughtful and insightful. I want to especially highlight the point you make that the subordinate clause I used shows why I made the statement that I did. That is an excellent point. The subordinate clause 'Since the first two miles are all uphill' provides context and background information that gives additional explanation related to the independent clause 'I suggest starting the race at an easy pace.'*

Other students in the class nod in agreement and I continue: "Next, I'm going to ask you to think about the impact of the subordinate clause in this sentence in a different way. This time, I'm going to ask you to think about how this sentence would be different if the subordinate clause was not used." I change the slide projected to the front of the room to one that depicts the original sentence "Since the first two miles are all uphill, I suggest starting the race at an easy pace" as well a revised version of the sentence that reads "I suggest starting the race at an easy pace." I read both versions to the students and explain

> *The first version of the sentence is the original one we discussed while the second version is a revised sentence with the subordinate clause 'since the*

first two miles are all uphill' removed. Without the subordinate clause, this sentence states 'I suggest starting the race at an easy pace.'

"Now that we've looked at both of these versions," I continue, please take two minutes and write a brief response to this question: How is the sentence different without the subordinate clause? After you write this response, share an idea with a partner. Then, we'll ask for volunteers to share ideas with the rest of the class.

As students share their ideas with partners, I move around the classroom, listen to their insights, and provide any relevant support. After that, I ask for volunteers to share their ideas. A student explains "The sentence is different without the subordinate clause because it doesn't say why you suggest starting the race at an easy pace. It doesn't have any explanation or detail."

"Great response," I reply.

You're absolutely right. The revised version of the sentence with the subordinate clause eliminated doesn't have the same level of explanation as the original one. As you said, this version doesn't indicate the reason to start the race at an easy pace.

Next, the students analyze the significance of the subordinate clause in the second example I showed them in our previous conversation. We review the sentence "I love the middle part of the race because there is a big, cheering crowd there" and the students reflect on why I used the subordinate clause "because there is a big, cheering crowd there." After that, the students reflect on how the sentence would be different if that subordinate clause was not used. Once they've thought carefully about these ideas and shared their insights about the significance of the subordinate clause in this sentence, I praise their work: "You have done such a great job of reflecting on the importance of the subordinate clauses I shared with you. Excellent work! Soon, you will be applying these same analytical skills to your own grammar inquiries!"

Instructional Recommendations

In this section, I share four instructional recommendations to use as you help your students reflect on the importance of the grammatical concepts you've shared with them:

1. Connect to the previous examples you've shared.
2. Create space for students to consider the importance of the concepts.

3. Provide support and follow-up explanations as students reflect on the concepts' importance.
4. Discuss with students that they will apply this same analytical approach to their own inquiries.

By using these recommendations, you'll engage your students in purposeful and meaningful learning activities that will help them understand what reflecting on the importance of a grammatical concept looks like and why it is a key part of the grammar inquiry experience. Now, let's take a look at each of these recommendations, examining how and why they can look in action.

Recommendation One: Connect to the Previous Examples You've Shared

To begin the process of reflecting on the importance of authentically used grammatical concepts, I recommend making a connection between this activity and the previous one, described in Chapter 2, in which you shared with students examples of authentically used grammatical concepts. To do so, I suggest reminding students that they recently looked at examples of grammatical concepts and then explaining that they will now be building on that activity by thinking about the importance of those grammatical concepts. Doing this activates students' prior knowledge and establishes a sense of continuity in their learning experiences. I like to begin this work by displaying the real-world grammatical concept that I shared with students in the previous activity and then explaining that, now that we've looked at this authentically used grammatical concept, we'll be thinking together about why it's important to the text in which it was used. For example, in the seventh-grade instructional example I shared earlier in this chapter that focused on the importance of strong verbs in a conversation about a football game, I shared the following explanation with my students:

> In our last class, we looked at examples of strong verbs in real-world situations. I showed you two examples of strong verbs from a recent conversation I had with one of my children about a Pittsburgh Steelers game. Today, we're going to think further about those examples: since we identified them in our last conversation, we're going to talk today about why those strong verb examples are so important.

This explanation was important to the students' learning experiences because it connected the work they had previously done with the analysis they were about to do. After this introductory statement, I reminded students of the examples we had discussed, which established the foundation for the analytical work that students would do. When beginning this instructional process with your students, I suggest providing the same type of introductory connection and reminder of the examples they had previously studied. This contextual information will set students up for success throughout the rest of their work.

Recommendation Two: Create Space for Students to Consider the Importance of the Concepts

Once you've activated students' prior knowledge about the authentic examples of grammatical concepts they've previously examined and introduced the analysis they'll do in their coming work, the next step is to create opportunities and space for students to consider the importance of the grammatical concepts to the texts in which they're used. As we've explored in this chapter, I recommend first asking students to consider why the creator of the text may have used the focal grammatical concept. This question calls for students to think metacognitively about the use of the grammatical concept by thinking about how the grammatical concept helped the text's creator achieve their objectives for the piece. For example, in the statement "Najee Harris sprinted past the defense!" that I shared with my seventh graders, the students, reflected on why the speaker may have used the strong verb "sprinted," commenting on how it clearly conveys the action being described. Similarly, in the text "Since the first two miles are all uphill, I suggest starting the race at an easy pace" which my tenth graders examined, they reflected on why I may have used the subordinate clause "Since the first two miles are all uphill" in the sentence. When creating space for your students to do similar analyses, I recommend first displaying the text containing the focal grammatical concept on a slide and then ask them to write individual reflections on why the text's creator may have used the focal grammatical concept. After that, I like to ask students to share their responses with a partner before finally asking for volunteers to share their insights with the whole class.

After students have shared their ideas on why the text's creator may have used the focal concept, I recommend asking them to consider how the text would be different if that concept was not used. In their responses to this question, students will compare the original text with a new version that does not contain it and present their own analyses of how the use of the discussed concept impacts the text. To facilitate this analysis with your students, I recommend displaying the original version of the text on a slide alongside a revised version with the focal grammatical concept either replaced by another word or removed entirely. In the instructional examples in this chapter, I replaced the strong verb "sprinted" with the weaker verb "went" in the seventh-grade example and removed the subordinate clause "Since the first two miles are all uphill" in the tenth-grade example. In both situations, students thought carefully about how the sentence was different without the identified example of its focal concept. Like with the previous analysis question, I suggest first asking students to write individual responses on how the sentence differed if the identified grammatical concept was not used. They then shared ideas, first with partners and then with the whole class. These opportunities to reflect on the importance of the grammatical concepts the class discussed helped students think deeply about the role of the focal concepts in effective real-world communication.

Recommendation Three: Provide Support and Follow-up Explanations as Students Reflect on the Concepts' Importance

When students reflect on the importance of the grammatical concepts they are analyzing, it's essential that we teachers provide them with support and with meaningful follow-up explanations. One way that I recommend supporting students as they consider the significance of the focal concepts is by moving around the classroom and listening to the students' responses as they share ideas with their peers. By doing this, you can get a sense of the students' understandings of the importance of the example they're analyzing and provide them with targeted support based on their specific responses. These conversations are great ways to clarify any misunderstandings of the topic that students have and to encourage them to think in more depth about the example they're analyzing. For example, when I was listening to a student share with a partner his thoughts on the importance of a subordinate clause, I noted that he did a good job of thinking in a general sense about the importance of subordinate clauses, but also encouraged him to go in more depth about the significance of the particular subordinate clause he was analyzing. I explained to this student, It's clear that you know why subordinate clauses are important, but I encourage you to think in even more specific detail about why the subordinate clause you're analyzing, which is "Since the first two miles are all uphill," is important to the sentence in which it's used and why it may have been used in the sentence we've examined.

After reflecting on this idea, the student shared a more detailed and specific response than he previously had.

Another way to facilitate students' success in this activity is to provide meaningful follow-up explanations when students share their reflections with the whole class. After students volunteer to share their insights on ideas such as why the creator of a text may have used the focal concept or how the text would be different if the concept wasn't used, we can use a graphic organizer to record key ideas from their responses. This allows us to highlight important points, explain why they're important, and visually display them in ways that are useful for all students in the class. The graphic organizer in

Reflection Questions	Statements from Student Observations	Summary Points to Share with Students
Why do you think the creator of the text used this example of the grammatical concept?		
How do you think the text would be different if the grammatical concept was not used?		

Figure 3.1 Grammatical Concept Discussion Graphic Organizer

Figure 3.1 is an example of this. (This figure is also available in Appendix B.) It lists the two key reflection questions discussed in this chapter— "Why do you think the creator of the text used this example of the grammatical concept?" and "How do you think the text would be different if the grammatical concept was not used?" In addition, it contains spaces to record statements from student observations and to list summary statements to share with students.

By using this graphic organizer, we can clearly convey to students highlights of the class discussion and other important takeaway points we want to emphasize to them, which can maximize their learning experiences about the significance of the focal concept.

Recommendation Four: Discuss with Students That They Will Apply This Same Analytical Approach to Their Own Inquiries

After students have thought carefully about the importance of authentically used grammatical concepts to the texts in which they appear, I recommend concluding this instructional process by talking with students about how they will apply this same approach to their own inquiries. In these discussions, I remind students of the meaningful analytical work they just did, emphasize why reflecting on the importance of authentically used grammatical concepts is a key part of understanding the purposeful grammar, and explain that they will be doing this same type of analytical work in their grammar inquiries with concepts they identify. When talking with my tenth graders about their analyses of the subordinate clauses I shared with them, I closed our conversation by emphasizing that the students would take this same approach to the analysis in their grammar inquiries: "You all did a great job today of thinking about the importance of subordinate clauses to the examples I showed you from conversation about running a race," I told them. Soon, you'll start on your own grammar inquiries, and you'll do this same type of analysis to examples of subordinate clauses you find in authentic situations in your own lives. You'll think about the importance of those subordinate clauses and use the analytical skills you utilized in our work today. I can't wait to see your work!

Key Takeaway Points

In this section, I identify key takeaway points to keep in mind as you work with your students to help them reflect on the importance of the authentically used grammatical concepts that you've shared with them.

- This step of the instructional process builds off of the previous learning experiences discussed in Chapter 2: after you've shown students real-world examples of grammatical concepts and helped them understand their features, you and your students can move to reflecting on the importance of those concepts to the texts in which they're used.
- There are two key aspects to these reflective discussions:
  - Discuss with students why the creator of the text may have used the concept.
  - Discuss with students how the text would be different if the concept was not used.
- Reflecting with students on the significance of authentically used grammatical concepts that we've shared and discussed with them is important to students' experiences with inquiry-based grammar instruction for two reasons:
  - It shows students the kind of analysis they will conduct in their own grammar inquiries.
  - It develops the analytical skills that students will apply to their own inquiries.
- When working with your students to help them reflect on the importance of the authentically used grammatical concepts that you've shared with them, I recommend following these instructional suggestions:

- Connect to the previous examples you've shared.
- Create space for students to consider the importance of the concepts.
- Provide support and follow-up explanations as students reflect on the concepts' importance.
- Discuss with students that they will apply this same analytical approach to their own inquiries.
◆ The infographic in Figure 3.2 provides a visual representation of these instructional recommendations.

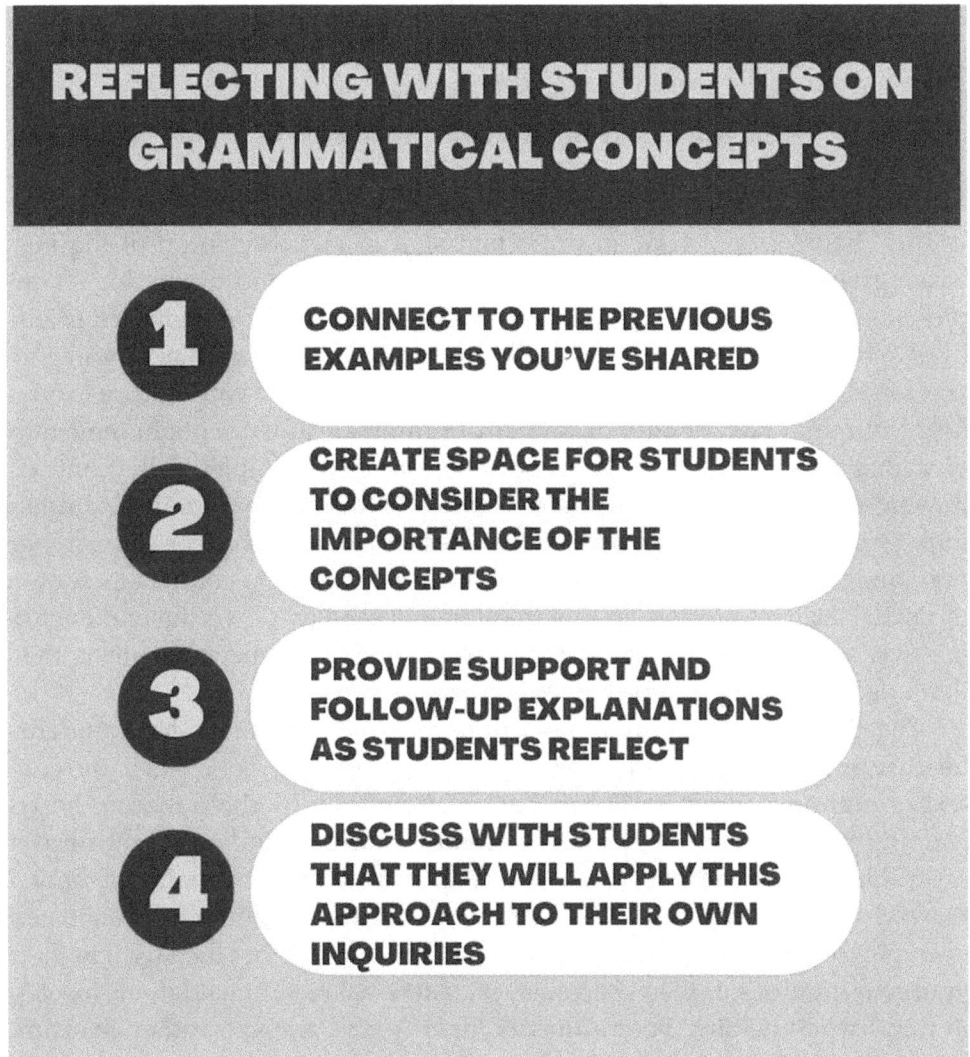

Figure 3.2 Infographic— Reflecting with Students on Grammatical Concepts

4

Helping Students Identify and Analyze Authentic Examples of Grammatical Concepts

In this chapter, we'll take an important step in our discussion of inquiry-based grammar instruction: we'll move from sharing and discussing examples of authentically used grammatical concepts that we've identified in our lives to helping students engage in their own inquiries. This chapter will give you ideas, explanations, examples, and suggestions that you can use as you help your students identify examples of grammatical concepts in their out-of-school lives and analyze the importance of those examples to the contexts in which they're used. When students move to this next part of the grammar inquiry process, they start to take what they've learned from the ideas in our previous chapters and use that knowledge as they begin to conduct their own inquiries. As we'll explore in this chapter, this is an empowering and engaging way for students to center their own experiences and interests as they think deeply about grammatical concepts!

The chapter begins with a description of what it means to help students identify and analyze authentic examples of grammatical concepts in the context of grammar inquiries. After that, it discusses why these inquiry-based learning activities are so important to students' understandings of the impact of grammatical concepts. Next, the chapter provides examples of how I worked with my seventh and tenth graders while they identified and analyzed examples of grammatical concepts from their own lives that they used in their grammar inquiries. It then shares key instructional recommendations to keep in mind when helping your students identify and analyze authentic examples of grammatical concepts for the grammar inquiries they are conducting.

DOI: 10.4324/9781003424260-5

Finally, it concludes with key closing points and a useful infographic. Now, let's explore this significant aspect of the grammar inquiry process!

What Is It?

At this stage of the grammar inquiry process, students move from the identification and analysis-related discussions they have had up to this point to truly embarking on their own inquiries. There are three related activities for students to do that will help them conduct these inquiries: 1) Review the essential question they'll explore in their inquiry, 2) Identify authentically used examples of the concept on which they're focusing, and 3) Analyze the importance of the grammatical concept they identified to the context in which it was used. In this section, we'll look at these components in detail, describing the key aspects of each one.

Review the Essential Question They'll Explore in Their Inquiry

Before students work on identifying and analyzing authentic examples of grammatical concepts, it's important that they review the essential question on which their inquiry is focused. These questions are thought-provoking, big-picture, and open-ended questions that call for students to think deeply about the real-world significance of the grammatical concept they're studying. Although the students have already been introduced to the essential question in the instructional activities discussed in Chapter 1: Building the Foundation for Inquiry-Based and Asset-Focused Grammar Instruction, this is a great time to remind students of the key question they'll be exploring in their inquiries and the information they need to understand as they answer that question. The essential questions students investigate provide them with a framework to use when finding and reflecting on authentically used grammatical concepts. I like to tell my students that their essential questions are the foundation for the work that they do in their identifications and analyses. I told my seventh graders during their inquiries on strong verbs that "Your essential question about strong verbs is the starting point for the strong verbs you'll identify and the analyses you'll share. By keeping that question in mind, you'll keep your inquiry focused." The essential question that guided the work these seventh graders did on strong verbs was "How do strong verbs make the texts we encounter outside of school as effective as possible?" and the essential question that the tenth graders described in this book examined was "Why are subordinate clauses important tools for communication in our everyday lives?" Reviewing with students the essential question that guides their inquiry can remind them of the ways they'll be thinking in deep and thoughtful ways about the grammatical concept they're studying and its importance to authentic communication.

Identify Authentically Used Examples of the Concept on Which They're Focusing

After students have reviewed their inquiry topics, they can begin to identify real-world examples of their focal grammatical concept. When I do this with my students, I first explore with them a variety of examples of everyday situations in which they might find the focal concept, such as verbal conversations, social media posts, text messages, song lyrics, books, and articles they read outside of school, song lyrics, movies, and television shows. I then ask students if they have any other ideas about possible situations in which they might identify that concept. After we've brainstormed these possible situations, I like to write the ideas that the students and I have shared on a piece of chart paper and post it in the classroom. This serves as a reminder and a resource for students to use as they look for examples of authentically used grammatical concepts.

Next, I ask students to explore the texts and situations of their choice with the goal of real-world examples of the focal concept. I create space in class for students to reflect and try to identify examples of the concept in their everyday lives, but I also ask them to take time outside of school to make these identifications. When my tenth graders were looking for examples of subordinate clauses in authentic communication, I emphasized to them the importance of taking time when they weren't at school to find real-world uses of that concept: "These real-world examples of subordinate clauses can be present in all kinds of situations," I told them.

> Keep this concept in mind in your communication outside of school and in the texts you encounter in all kinds of situations. This will help you conduct a grammar inquiry that addresses the essential question and is authentic to you.

Analyze the Importance of the Grammatical Concept They Identified to the Context in which it Was Used

Once students have identified authentic examples of the grammatical concept they're focusing on in their inquiries, the next step is for them to analyze the importance of that concept. During these analyses, students think carefully about the importance of the concept they've identified to the context in which it was used. For example, if a student found an example of a subordinate clause in a social media post, they would reflect on the importance of that subordinate clause to the information in the post and to the post's effectiveness. When students conduct these analyses, I like to ask them to reflect on the two topics they considered in the analytical work described in Chapter

3: 1) Why the creator of the text may have used the concept, and 2) How the text would be different if the concept was not used. This builds off the knowledge and analytical skills developed in the previous activity, in which they reflected on these topics regarding a teacher-identified example. To help students reflect on and analyze the importance of the grammatical concepts they identified, I like to use the graphic organizer depicted in Figure 4.1, which contains space for the example the student found, the context in which it was used, the student's reflection on why the text's creator may have used the concept, and their analysis of how the text would be different if the concept was not used. (This graphic organizer is also available in Appendix B.)

Grammatical Concept Example	Context In Which It Was Used	Why the Text's Creator May Have Used the Concept	How the Text Would Be Different If the Concept Was Not Used

Figure 4.1 Grammatical Concept Analysis Graphic Organizer

By reflecting on these topics, students will engage in careful reflection on the significance of the authentically used grammatical concepts they found, which is a key part of their grammar inquiries.

Why Is It Important?

The process of students identifying and analyzing authentic examples of grammatical concepts is important for two particularly significant reasons. By engaging in these identifications and analyses, students will 1) Think deeply about the grammatical concept they're studying, and 2) Work with grammar in asset-based ways. In this section, we'll look closely at each of these reasons why identifying and analyzing real-world usage of grammatical concepts is important to students' learning experiences, reflecting on what each of these ideas means and why it is significant.

Students Think Deeply about the Grammatical Concept They're Studying

When students identify and analyze real-world examples of a specific grammatical concept, they engage with that concept in deep and analytical ways. This is especially significant because grammar instruction has traditionally focused on the memorization of terms and out-of-context worksheets (Weaver, 1998). In contrast, the identification and analysis of real-world examples of grammatical concepts described in this chapter moves students well beyond memorization and worksheets. First, it calls for them to examine their authentic communication to find examples of the focal concept. This practice extends students' learning outside of traditional school-based texts and requires them to think carefully about language used in a variety of situations, creating more opportunities to engage with the material. Second, this work involves students thinking carefully and analytically about the impact of the real-world examples of grammar use that they've identified. The combination of these practices creates in-depth learning experiences for students that build strong understandings of the focal concept.

Students Work with Grammar in Asset-Based Ways

In addition to calling for students to think deeply about their focal grammatical concept, identifying and analyzing authentic examples of grammar is important because it incorporates students' assets. As mentioned in this book's introduction, asset-based instruction approaches teaching, learning, and assessment in ways that focus on real-world connections to classroom material and meaningful applications of students' knowledge (New York

University, 2020) and creates opportunities for students to demonstrate their understandings in authentic and relevant ways (Ruday & Caprino, 2022). By engaging in grammar inquiries that incorporate their real-world communication experiences, students make meaningful connections to authentic language use and showcase their knowledge in relevant ways. This contrasts with deficit-based approaches to grammar instruction, which focus primarily on factual recall and out-of-context assessment. For example, when students find examples of strong verbs in their everyday lives, identify those examples, and reflect on their importance, they share their understandings of the topic in ways that center authentic applications of their knowledge of what strong verbs are, why they are important, and how they are used in students' real-world communication. Identifying and analyzing real-world examples of grammatical concept use prioritizes students' assets and centers their unique individual experiences.

How Can It Look in Action?

Now, let's look together at classroom examples of how I helped students in my seventh- and tenth-grade English classes identify and analyze authentic examples of grammatical concepts. In these descriptions, you'll see how I supported students in these classes as they found and discussed examples of grammatical concepts related to their inquiries that they encountered in their everyday lives. First, let's take a look inside a seventh-grade classroom and check out the strong verb identification and analysis that was done there.

"I'm so excited for today!" I enthusiastically greet my seventh graders as they enter the room.

> Today we take an important step in our grammar inquiries. In our last class, we reviewed our essential question, 'How do strong verbs make the texts we encounter outside of school as effective as possible?', brainstormed some situations in which we can find strong verbs in our out-of-school lives, and began to think about possible examples of strong verbs in authentic, real-world situations.

"Now," I continue,

> we're going to build off those experiences by talking about your identifications and analyses of the strong verbs you've found. I'm going to give each of you a graphic organizer that asks you to list the strong verb you found,

write the context in which it was used, share your thoughts on why the text's creator may have used that strong verb, and then write how you think the text would be different if that strong verb wasn't used.

I project the Grammatical Concept Analysis Graphic Organizer depicted earlier in this chapter in Figure 4.1 to the front of the room and give each student a paper copy of it.

"As you work on recording your identifications and analyses on this graphic organizer," I tell the students, "I will check in with you to see how you're doing, answer any questions you have, and help you as you do this important work."

I circulate the classroom, checking in with students as they work. One of the students with whom I confer is analyzing the strong verb "devoured" in a conversation about a dog eating food. I sit down next to the student and ask how he's doing. "I'm doing great," he replies cheerfully. *I have a really good example of a strong verb. My example is 'devoured.' My brother said it when he was watching our dog eat one evening. My brother was looking at the dog and said 'He must have been really hungry. He just devoured all of that food I just put in his bowl.'*

"That's a great example," I respond. *I love how you picked such a strong verb that you encountered in a real-world situation. Let's think now about the next part of the graphic organizer that asks why the text's creator, in this case, your brother, may have used the grammatical concept. Why do you think he used the strong verb 'devoured' in this situation?*

"I think he used it to show the way our dog ate," the student replies. *Our dog ate the food really quickly and without looking up, or taking a break, or anything like that. I think my brother used that strong verb to show the way our dog ate the food and to show how hungry he must have been to eat like that.*

"That's such a wonderful analysis," I say, praising the student.

I love the way that you commented in specific ways about why your brother used a strong verb in this statement. You did a good job of analyzing what your brother may have wanted to show about this situation and why the strong verb was important to the message he wanted to get across—the specific way your dog ate and how hungry he was. Now, let's think about the final category on the graphic organizer: how do you think this text would be different if your brother didn't use the strong verb 'devoured' and used a weaker and more general verb like 'ate' instead?

"If he had done that," the student answered,

the sentence would be really different. Even though you would still know that the dog had his food, you wouldn't know how he had it. The strong verb tells exactly how our dog ate his food. Also, the thing that my brother said wouldn't make as much sense if he used a weaker verb like 'ate.' He started by saying that the dog was really hungry and then said that he 'devoured' the food. The strong verb 'devoured' shows how you can tell that the dog was hungry. If my brother said 'ate' instead, you wouldn't be able to tell that the dog was hungry from the information in the sentence. The strong 'devoured' shows how our dog ate his food and shows that he was really hungry. You wouldn't really know this without the strong verb.

"Outstanding work," I exclaim, praising the student's thoughtful and insightful response. "I love how carefully you reflected on this statement and the way you thought in depth about the significance of the concept." I then conferred with other students in the class, monitoring their progress, noting the strengths of their identifications and analyses, and providing support when needed. After I confer with the students, I ask them to talk with partners about their identifications and analyses. Then, at the end of class, I address the students: "You all did such wonderful work today on identifying and analyzing authentic examples of strong verbs. Great job!"

Now, let's see inside a tenth-grade English classroom and examine the identification and analysis of subordinate clauses that accompanied those students' grammar inquiries.

The energy in the tenth-grade English class fills the air. Students are using the graphic organizer depicted in Figure 4.1 to record their identifications and analyses of subordinate clauses. As I circulate the room, I can tell from the students' focused work on their graphic organizers, the detailed responses they write, and the quickness with which they all begin working that they are fully engaged in this activity, which corresponds with their grammar inquiry question "Why are subordinate clauses important tools for communication in our everyday lives?"

"I love how excited you are about this work," I tell the students as I smile.

You all are doing such a great job of thinking about the subordinate clause you found, the context in which it was used, why you think the text's creator may have used that subordinate clause, and how you think the text would be different if the subordinate clause wasn't used. I'm going to come around and confer with as many of you as I can about your work. If I don't get to confer with you today, I will talk with you in our coming classes as we continue to work on our inquiries. I can't wait to see your identifications and analyses of authentically used subordinate clauses.

I sit down next to a student and begin to confer with him. He eagerly begins the conference by sharing with the subordinate clause that he identified: "I was looking through my text messages and I found a subordinate clause that I thought would be great for my grammar inquiry about why subordinate clauses are important to *communication in our everyday lives. I picked this text message that I sent to my friends: 'Since I got a Five Guys gift card for my birthday, fries are on me!' That's the subordinate that I'm using for my inquiry. It's a great subordinate clause, and my friends and I love the fries at Five Guys,"* the student smiles, referring to a popular restaurant that serves hamburgers and french fries, among other foods

"That's a great example," I share with the student. "I love how you identified an authentic, real-world example of a subordinate clause that you used when communicating with your friends. It's an excellent example of subordinate clause use. Great job sharing it. Also, I love Five Guys' fries also!" I continue, grinning. "Now, let's talk about the next two parts of the graphic organizer: why the text's creator may have used the subordinate clause and how the text would be different if the subordinate clause was not used."

The student responds, "Yeah, I thought a lot about both of those. I'm the text's creator and I used the subordinate clause to explain why the fries are on me. It explains why I'm getting the fries for everyone by telling them that I'm doing it since I received a Five Guys gift card for my birthday."

"Great insight," I interject.

"Thanks," says the student, continuing his explanation.

For the part about how the text would be different if the subordinate clause wasn't used, I think that the sentence wouldn't have any explanation. It would just say 'Fries are on me.' This is a much more basic sentence and doesn't explain why I'm saying that the fries are on me. I think the sentence with the subordinate clause is so much better because of all of the explanation that it gives.

"Wonderful job!" I praise the student's thoughtful work.

You did a great job in all parts of that explanation. You identified an authentic subordinate clause that you used and then reflected in very insightful ways about the significance of the subordinate clause and how different the sentence would be without the subordinate clause that you used. The insights you shared about how different the sentence would be without it really showed me your knowledge of the importance of the subordinate clause in the text message. Great work!

Instructional Recommendations

Here I present four instructional recommendations to use as you help your students identify and analyze authentic examples of grammatical concepts for their grammar inquiries:

1. Establish a connection between this work and what students have already done.
2. Help students review the grammar inquiry essential question.
3. Brainstorm with students situations in which they could find authentic examples of their focal concept.
4. Confer with students as they work on their identifications and analyses.

These suggestions will help you provide your students with a combination of support and independence as they do the important work of identifying and analyzing real-world examples of grammatical concepts that align with their grammar inquiries. Now, let's take a look at each of the recommendations in detail.

Recommendation One: Establish a Connection between This Work and What Students Have Already Done

To help students feel comfortable with and prepared to succeed on this activity, I like to take some time to establish a connection between what they will do and what they have already done in the previously described instructional practices. To do so, I remind students of our initial discussions of the features and importance of the focal grammatical concept, and I discuss with them the work they recently did when they looked at examples of authentically used grammatical concepts that I showed them and then reflected on those concepts' importance. I have found that doing so activates students' prior knowledge on thinking carefully about real-world examples of grammatical concepts and helps them feel comfortable as they begin to work on their own inquiries.

For example, to help prepare my seventh graders for their work identifying and analyzing authentic examples of strong verbs, I reviewed with them the variety of activities we had already done with this concept. "We've done so much great work with strong verbs, and that has prepared you to do the identification and analysis that you'll do next," I told them.

> We've talked about what strong verbs are and why they're important. We've also looked at published examples of them. In addition, in our most recent work with strong verbs, you looked at examples of strong verbs that I shared with you from a conversation I had with one of my children about a football game, discussed why they're strong verbs, and analyzed their importance. Now, you're going to do this work on your own by conducting your own grammar inquiries. You'll find a strong verb in your authentic communication and analyze its importance. This activity will build off of everything that we've done so far with real-world uses of grammatical concepts.

By sharing explanations and connections like these with students, we establish a clear connection between all of the work they've done up to that point. This reviews for students the work they've done and helps them see how these instructional activities build on each other to facilitate their success.

Recommendation Two: Help Students Review the Grammar Inquiry Essential Question

Once you've connected the work that students will do on this activity with their previous activities and learning experiences, I recommend helping students review one more piece of information with them: the essential questions that will guide their grammar inquiries. Although students have already seen these questions when they were introduced to their grammar inquiries, it's important to review the questions at this stage when students are about to begin to identify and analyze examples of the focal concept in their out-of-school lives. As I shared earlier in this chapter, I tell my students that it's important that they understand and keep in mind their essential questions in order to keep their inquiries focused.

When I help students review an essential question, I address two key ideas: what the essential question is and why it's important. For example, when I talked with my tenth graders about the question "Why are subordinate clauses important tools for communication in our everyday lives?" that guided their inquiries, I first made sure that students understood the key aspects of the question. To do so, I revisited the key components of subordinate clauses, discussed their role in everyday communication, and explained that the question is asking them to consider why subordinate clauses they encounter in real-world situations are important to the texts in which they're used. After that, I talked with the students about why considering this question could be important and meaningful to their knowledge of the concept and to their awareness of effective language use. "This question is important," I shared with the students, because it helps us think about how subordinate clauses are used and why they play a major role in communication. When you work on this grammar inquiry and answer this question, you'll look at real-world ways that subordinate clauses are used and the impact of using them.

Recommendation Three: Brainstorm with Students Situations in Which They Could Find Authentic Examples of Their Focal Concept

After you've talked with students about the characteristics and importance of their essential questions and are comfortable with their awareness of it, I recommend working with students to brainstorm situations where they could find authentic examples of their grammatical concept. During these conversations, I emphasize to students that they can find grammatical concepts in any situation in which language is used. Once we've established this, the discussion typically becomes a fun activity in which we discuss a wide range of communication contexts and talk about how the focal concept could appear in those situations. As mentioned previously in this chapter, I identify a wide range of contexts in which a focal concept could potentially be used and then I ask students to contribute other ideas.

Once we've listed a number of different situations in which someone might use the focal grammatical concept, we review the list and talk together about potential ways that concept might play an important role. For example, if the focal concept is subordinate clauses and a possible text is song lyrics, we discuss reasons why a songwriter might use a subordinate clause, highlighting ideas such as how a subordinate clause could give background information that might explain why the singer is feeling the way they are. As you and your students discuss these potential situations, I recommend recording them on a piece of chart paper and posting it in the classroom for students to return to as they work. This provides students with a resource to which they can return as they consider possible authentic communication situations in which they might find examples of a grammatical concept.

Recommendation Four: Confer with Students as They Work on Their Identifications and Analyses

Now that you've prepared students to conduct inquiries into authentic uses of grammatical concepts using the ideas discussed in the first three recommendations, my final suggestion is to confer with students as they identify and analyze examples of the focal concepts they've found in their out-of-school lives. To do this, I suggest asking students to use the authentically used grammatical concept they've identified to complete the graphic organizer depicted in Figure 4.1. As explained earlier in this chapter, the graphic organizer asks students to identify the grammatical concept example they've found, state the context in which it was used, reflect on why the text's creator may have used the concept, and comment on how the text would be different if the concept was not used. While students complete the graphic organizer, I like to check in with them to monitor their progress, note strengths of their existing work, and provide them with any needed support. These conferences present opportunities to give students individualized feedback on the work they have done up to that point on their grammar inquiries, an especially fitting feature given the student-centered and individual-oriented approach to teaching and learning that is central to grammar inquiries.

Key Takeaway Points

This section shares key takeaway points to keep in mind as you help your students identify and analyze authentic examples of grammatical concepts.

- At this stage of the grammar inquiry process, students move from the identification and analysis-related discussions they have had up to this point to truly embarking on their own inquiries.
- There are three related activities for students to do that will help them conduct these inquiries:
  - Review the essential question they'll explore in their inquiry.
  - Identify authentically used examples of the concept on which they're focusing.
  - Analyze the importance of the grammatical concept they identified to the context in which it was used.
- The process of students identifying and analyzing authentic examples of grammatical concepts is important for two particularly significant reasons. By engaging in these identifications and analyses, students will:
  - Think deeply about the grammatical concept they're studying.
  - Work with grammar in asset-based ways.
- When working with your students to help them identify and analyze authentic examples of grammatical concepts, I recommend following these instructional recommendations:
  - Establish a connection between this work and what students have already done.
  - Help students review the grammar inquiry essential question.
  - Brainstorm with students situations in which they could find authentic examples of their focal concept.
  - Confer with students as they work on their identifications and analyses.
- The infographic in Figure 4.2 depicts these instructional recommendations.

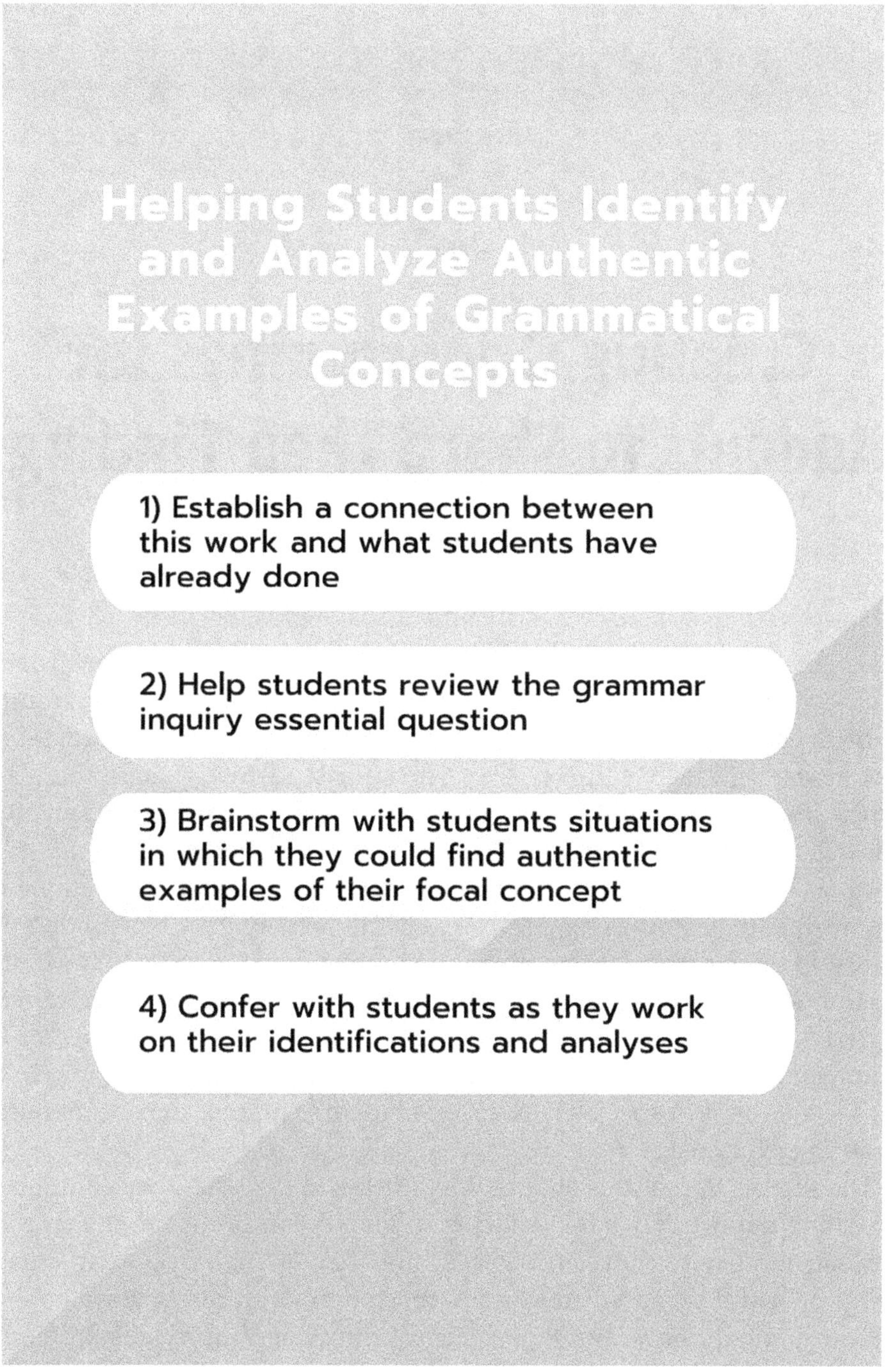

Helping Students Identify and Analyze Authentic Examples of Grammatical Concepts

1) Establish a connection between this work and what students have already done

2) Help students review the grammar inquiry essential question

3) Brainstorm with students situations in which they could find authentic examples of their focal concept

4) Confer with students as they work on their identifications and analyses

Figure 4.2 Infographic—Helping Students Identify and Analyze Authentic Examples of Grammatical Concepts

5

Creating Opportunities for Students to Share Their Findings

This chapter explores the next step of inquiry-based grammar instruction: creating opportunities for students to share the findings of their grammar inquiries and setting them up for success as they do so. The information in this chapter will help you construct ways for students to share the results of their inquiries and will guide you as you communicate to students what they will need to do to successfully share that information. This part of the grammar inquiry process is the time when students give presentations that demonstrate their knowledge of the essential question that has guided their inquiry. In these presentations, students support their response to the inquiry question with an example of an authentically used grammatical concept that they have each identified and with a discussion of the importance of that grammatical concept to the text in which it appears. As we'll consider in this chapter, this is an especially exciting, student-centered, and academically rewarding experience!

The first section of this chapter identifies and discusses key components of creating opportunities for students to give presentations that share their grammar inquiry findings. After that, the chapter addresses why creating these opportunities is so important to students' grammar inquiry experiences, highlighting ways that sharing grammar inquiry results centers students in their learning experiences and helps make the work culturally relevant and sustaining. Then, the chapter shares examples of how I worked with my seventh- and tenth-grade English classes to create meaningful and well-organized opportunities for them to share their inquiry findings. Next,

DOI: 10.4324/9781003424260-6

it shares key recommendations to consider as you create opportunities for students to share the findings of their grammar inquiries before concluding with key closing points and an infographic to refer back to as you put the ideas discussed in this chapter into action. Let's now explore together how to create opportunities for students to share their grammar inquiry findings!

What Is It?

At this point in the grammar inquiry process, our instructional focus turns to constructing opportunities for students to effectively share the findings of their grammar inquiries, which they do by giving presentations that describe their responses to the inquiry's essential question, the authentic example of the focal grammatical concept they identified, and their analysis of the important of that grammatical concept to the text in which it was used. There are two especially significant aspects of constructing these opportunities for students: 1) Organizing community events where students will share the results of their inquiries, and 2) Providing students with clear guidelines for sharing their findings. Let's look at each of these components individually, examining key information associated with each one.

Organizing Community Events Where Students Will Share the Results of Their Inquiries

I believe that grammar inquiries are most effectively shared with authentic audiences that go beyond the teacher and even the other students in the class as well. Since grammar inquiries focus on the language that students encounter in their authentic communication, and this authentic communication can include many individuals in students' lives and communities, I like to organize community-oriented events for students to share their grammar inquiry results through presentations that describe what they learned in their inquiries. When planning for these events, I invite other English classes in the school and students' caregivers to attend, and I make a flyer for students to share with and invite others that they would like to attend. Students have invited family friends, extended relatives, and others who are important to them, such as sports coaches, mentors, and theater teachers. Figure 5.1 depicts a flyer infographic that I created for my seventh-graders' strong verb grammar inquiry presentations. I gave the flyer to other English teachers and administrators in the school, sent it to students' caregivers, and provided copies for students to distribute to anyone else in their communities or out-of-school lives that they would like to invite.

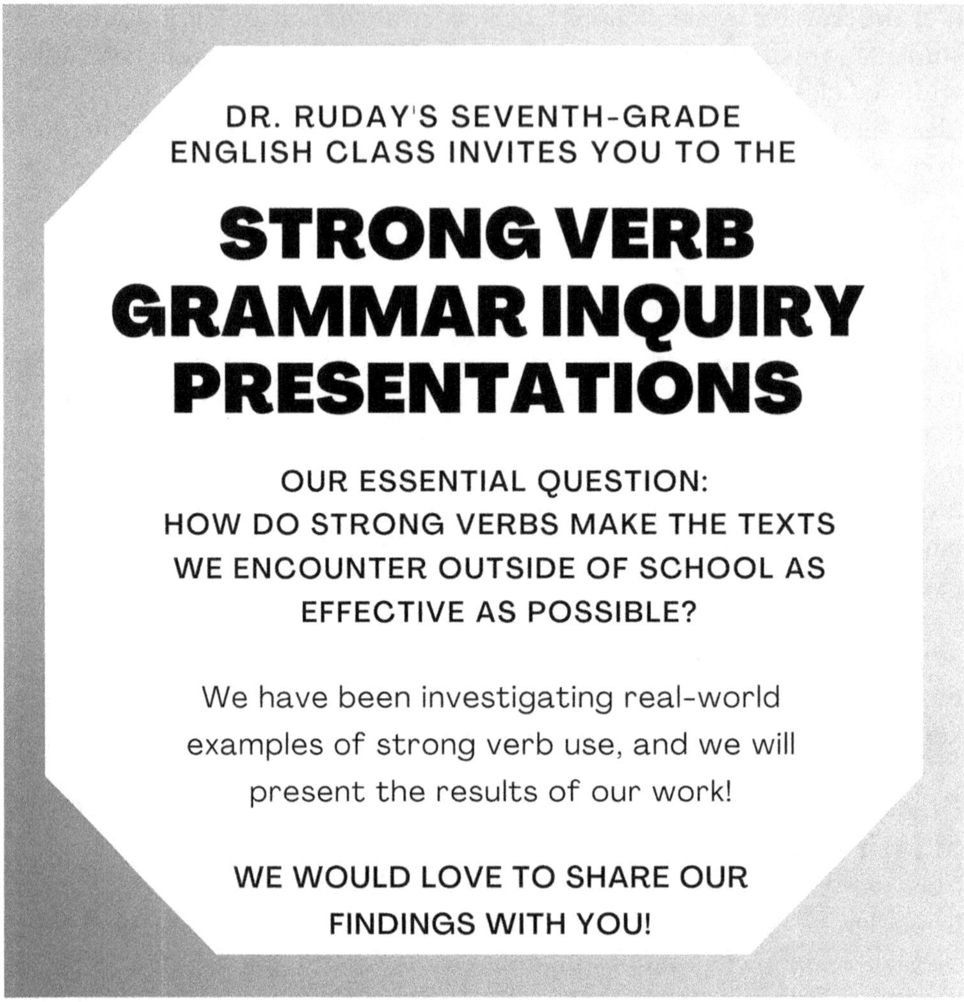

> DR. RUDAY'S SEVENTH-GRADE
> ENGLISH CLASS INVITES YOU TO THE
>
> # STRONG VERB GRAMMAR INQUIRY PRESENTATIONS
>
> OUR ESSENTIAL QUESTION:
> HOW DO STRONG VERBS MAKE THE TEXTS WE ENCOUNTER OUTSIDE OF SCHOOL AS EFFECTIVE AS POSSIBLE?
>
> We have been investigating real-world examples of strong verb use, and we will present the results of our work!
>
> **WE WOULD LOVE TO SHARE OUR FINDINGS WITH YOU!**

Figure 5.1 Grammar Inquiry Presentation Flyer Example

Before the students give their presentations, I share some introductory remarks with the audience, providing them with an overview of the grammar inquiry project and explaining what to expect when the students present. In addition, I talk directly with the students before they share their inquiries, telling them that I'm proud of the work they did on their inquiries and that they should view the day as an opportunity to show off all of the knowledge and insights they've gained while they worked on this project. We huddle together like before a sporting event and get excited about the wonderful ideas that everyone in the class will share. Before my tenth graders shared their inquiry results, I told them:

Everyone here has done wonderful work on the subordinate clause grammar inquiries. You've found so many examples of real-world subordinate clauses and have done a great job of analyzing their importance. I'm so proud of you and I can't wait for everyone here to see the results of the great work you've done. Team subordinate clauses, let's go!

Providing Students with Clear Guidelines for Sharing Their Findings

Another essential component of creating opportunities for students to share the findings of their grammar inquiries is providing them with clear guidelines to follow when doing so. When communicating these guidelines to students, I focus on providing them with concrete expectations for what I want them to do and express when they present their inquiry results. To do so, I give students a guideline sheet that identifies key aspects of their inquiry presentations. For example, before my tenth graders shared the findings of their subordinate clause grammar inquiries, I gave them the document depicted in Figure 5.2.

This guidelines sheet provides students with clear expectations for their work, maximizing their abilities to successfully deliver informative and focused presentations on their grammar inquiry findings that align with the project's essential question. While the specific concepts and corresponding essential questions will vary based on the particular grammatical topics, the key components of the guidelines (such as the presentation length, slide information, connection to the essential question, identification, and analysis) will be consistent across different grammar inquiries. When I share the guidelines with students, I explain to them that this information will help them share their inquiry findings in the most effective ways possible. As I told my tenth graders "These guidelines are here to support you and help you give the best grammar inquiry presentation you can. I am very excited to see your excellent presentations!"

Why Is It Important?

Creating opportunities for students to share their grammar inquiry findings is an especially significant aspect of this process and of the experience that it can create for students. It creates opportunities for students not only to share the results of inquiries that represent their authentic experiences with grammatical concepts, but also to share those ideas with a wide audience that goes

> **Subordinate Clause Grammar Inquiry Presentation Guidelines**
>
> Soon, you will present the findings from your grammar inquiries!
>
> To do so, you will give a presentation on your work on the grammar inquiry project.
>
> Here are some guidelines to follow to help you have a successful presentation:
>
> - The presentation should be three to five minutes long.
> - It should include slides that contain text and relevant images.
> - The presentation content should relate to the grammar inquiry essential question: "Why are subordinate clauses important tools for communication in our everyday lives?"
> - The presentation should identify an example of a subordinate clause you identified in your everyday life.
> - In the presentation, you should analyze the importance of the subordinate clause you identified by discussing why the text's creator may have used the subordinate clause and how the text would be different if the subordinate clause was not used.
> - The presentation should have a concluding section that connects your subordinate clause identification and analysis with the essential question.
>
> Just let me know if you have any questions! I am excited to see the great presentations you share!

Figure 5.2 Grammar Inquiry Presentation Guidelines Example

beyond the traditional classroom and into aspects of the students' communities. There are three reasons why the action of students presenting their findings in the ways described in this chapter is especially important: it makes the experience meaningful for students; it is motivational for them; and it is aligned with the values of grammar inquiries. In this section, we'll explore each of these ideas individually.

The Experience is Meaningful for Students

The opportunity to share examples of grammatical concepts they encounter in their out-of-school lives, and to present that information to a wide audience that includes not only the teacher, but also classmates, other students in the school, caregivers, and community members, provides a meaningful learning experience for students through its authentic approach. This authenticity comes in part from the fact that students are working and engaging with real-world examples and concepts, creating an opportunity for students to see the grammatical concepts they study as relevant and meaningful to their real-world communication. The meaningful nature of this experience also comes from the wide, community-based audience and the opportunity that it provides students to share relevant information with that audience. Through these opportunities to engage with relevant content and to share their findings with audiences that go beyond the teacher and extend to students' broader communities, students can have a meaningful experience sharing their inquiry results.

The Experience is Motivating for Students

The components of grammar inquiry presentations that create meaningful experiences—authentic connections to students' out-of-school lives and audiences that incorporate aspects of their communities—can help increase student motivation (Fletcher & Portalupi, 2001). Assessment practices that incorporate students' assets (in this case, by connecting grammatical concepts to their out-of-school lives and including a community-based presentation) by honoring their "preferences, identities, and cultures" (Ruday & Caprino, 2022, p. 16). By selecting examples of concepts that are relevant to them and align with their out-of-school literacy practices, students can incorporate aspects of their preferences, identities, and cultures as they convey what they've learned about their grammar inquiry essential questions. A student in my seventh-grade class commented on how the content and audience of the grammar inquiry presentations motivated him to do his best work: I liked that I could share a strong verb example from my life and that so many people, not just people in the school, came to watch us present. I wanted to do a really good job because I was sharing something that mattered to me to so many people.

The Experience is Aligned with the Values of Grammar Inquiries

A final reason that the experience of presenting real-world examples of grammatical concepts to community-based audiences is so important that it aligns with the essential values of grammar inquiries. As discussed in this book's introduction, inquiry-based grammar instruction values students' assets and experiences (New York University, 2020), incorporates thought-provoking essential questions (McTighe & Wiggins, 2013), and is focused on making grammar instruction culturally relevant (Ladson-Billings, 1995) and culturally sustaining (Paris, 2012). When students share their grammar inquiry findings, they are demonstrating their knowledge in ways that are aligned with the key principles that have informed their experiences with the entire grammar inquiry project. The experience of sharing inquiry findings discussed in this chapter aligns with students' previous instructional experiences and activities while also centering their unique perspectives in the assessment process. The National Council of Teachers of English (2018) document "Literacy Assessment: Definitions, Principles, and Practices" emphasizes the importance of assessments being aligned with "their classroom learning context" (para. 5). This assessment experience aligns with the context and values of students' grammar inquiries, maximizing its meaning and relevance for students.

How Can It Look in Action?

In this section, we'll look at two instructional examples related to students sharing their grammar inquiries. In the information shared here, you'll see inside the events at which students shared their inquiry results, checking out descriptions of these events and examples of student work shared at each one. First, let's check out the event at which students in my seventh-grade class shared their strong verb inquiry findings.

"Welcome, everyone," I said to all of the people who filled the seventh-grade English classroom.

> *I know you're all here to see our students present their grammar inquiry presentations on strong verbs. They have worked very hard on this project and have learned a lot while also thinking in new ways about strong verbs and their importance. As a class, we investigated the essential question 'How do strong verbs make the texts we encounter outside of school as effective as possible?' The students did an outstanding job of thinking carefully about this question. In the presentations you'll see today, each student will share their answer to this question. That answer will be informed for each student by an identification of a strong verb they identified in their out-of-school experiences and by an analysis of the importance of that strong verb. These students are so excited to share their great work with you!*

Before the students give their presentations, I huddle the group together and tell them how proud I am of their work: "You all have done such wonderful work on your strong verb grammar inquiries. You've thought so carefully about the importance of strong verbs to all kinds of texts we encounter outside of school, and that hard work has shown up in your great identifications and analyses. Go out there and show everyone your wonderful ideas!"

We count down—"one, two, three"—with our hands in the middle of the huddle and then cheer before the students present.

One of the first to present is the student whose identification and analysis of the strong verb 'devoured' was discussed in Chapter 4. During his presentation, he explained, "I identified the strong verb 'devoured' in a conversation with my brother about our dog eating. My brother was talking about the dog and said 'He must have been really hungry. He just devoured all of that food I just put in his bowl.' This strong verb was really important because it showed the exact way our dog ate his food and how hungry he was. If he didn't use that strong verb, and used a weaker verb like 'ate' instead, you wouldn't know that our dog was so hungry."

The student continued to explain, "Finding and analyzing this strong verb in my everyday life really helped me understand the essential question 'How do strong verbs make the texts we encounter outside of school as effective as possible?' I really understand now that strong verbs are important to what we do outside of school because they help people say really clearly what happened."

When sharing this insight about his identification and analysis of the strong verb "devoured" and its connection to the essential question that guided the students' grammar inquiries, this student displays the slide depicted in Figure 5.3.

Throughout the presentation sessions, other students shared similarly thoughtful ideas and insights about the importance of strong verbs and how their inquiries helped them understand the role of this concept in the texts we encounter in

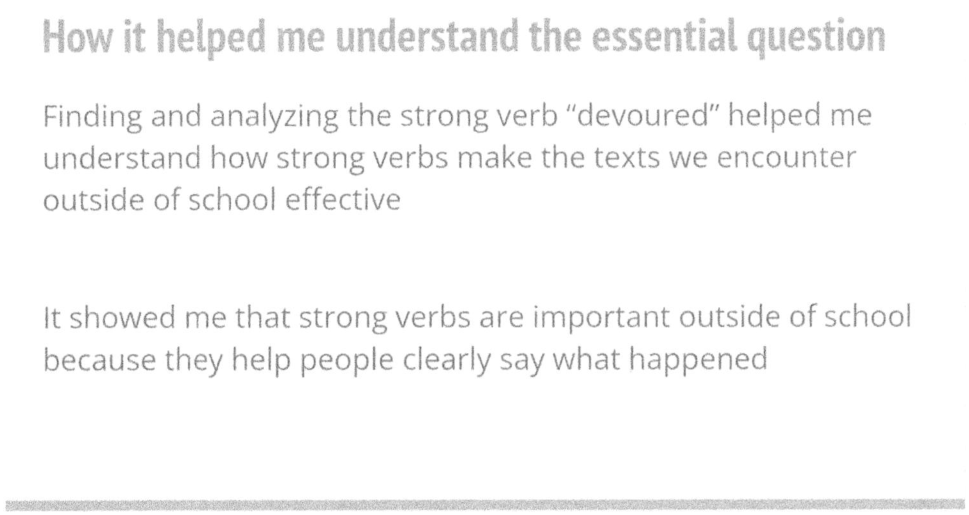

How it helped me understand the essential question

Finding and analyzing the strong verb "devoured" helped me understand how strong verbs make the texts we encounter outside of school effective

It showed me that strong verbs are important outside of school because they help people clearly say what happened

Figure 5.3 Student Presentation Example: Strong Verb Analysis

authentic situations. Once the sessions had ended, I addressed the audience again: "Thank you all for coming today, and congratulations to our wonderful students for their thoughtful ideas. Let's give them all a hand."

Let's now look inside the event at which tenth-grade students shared the results of their subordinate clause inquiries.

The energy in the tenth-grade English classroom is high. The guests in attendance include students and teachers from other English classes in the school, students' caregivers, siblings, other relatives, sports coaches, former teachers, family friends, and others who are connected to students' lives in various ways. There is a strong sense of connection here to students' out-of-school lives and communities, which is exactly what the grammar inquiry project is designed to create. "This is such a wonderful event," I tell the students and guests, "because of the way the students' out-of-school lives and communities are represented in so many ways." I continue to explain,

> *Those authentic, community-based connections can be seen in the subordinate clause examples that you, the students, have identified and analyzed. In addition, these connections are evident because of all of the wonderful guests from the students' lives and communities that are here in support today. Thanks to you all for your contributions to our day today.*

The student whose ideas about a subordinate clause in a text message about Five Guys restaurant were featured in Chapter 4 steps to the front of the room and begins to present. He shares his identification of the subordinate clause "Since I got a Five Guys gift card for my birthday" in the text message he sent to his friends that read "Since I got a Five Guys gift card for my birthday, fries are on me!" After sharing this identification, he presents his analysis of the importance of the subordinate clause to the text message in which it was used. Included in his discussion of the significance of this subordinate clause is the statement

> *This subordinate clause plays a very important role in the text message that I sent. I used the subordinate clause 'since I got a Five Guys gift card for my birthday' to give background information and explanation for my statement 'fries are on me.' This background information and explanation is significant because it helps my friends who received the text message understand the situation and know exactly why I'm offering fries. The gift card made it possible for me to offer them fries and the subordinate clause communicates that.*

The student continues to explain,

> *If I didn't use the subordinate clause, the message would not have the background information and explanation it has. It would say 'fries are on me,' but it wouldn't say why, which might have been kind of confusing to my friends.*

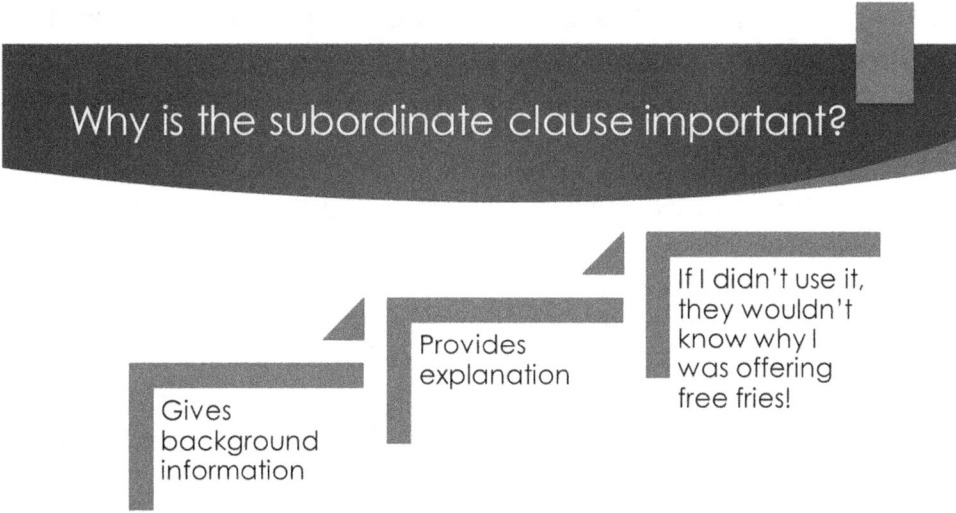

Figure 5.4 Student Presentation Example: Subordinate Clause Analysis

I mean, I offer them fries sometimes, but I don't always just go around buying people fries, he laughs. "Without the subordinate clause, they wouldn't know why I'm buying these fries for them."

While sharing this explanation of the importance of the subordinate clause he identified, the student displays the slide depicted in Figure 5.4, which highlights key components of this explanation.

Instructional Recommendations

In this section, I describe four instructional suggestions to keep in mind as you create opportunities for students to share their grammar inquiry findings. The recommendations discussed here are:

1. Reach out to community members about the grammar inquiry presentations.
2. Emphasize to students that grammar inquiry presentations are opportunities to share real-world ideas with authentic audiences.
3. Provide students with clear guidelines for their grammar inquiry presentations.
4. Purposefully address guests and students before grammar inquiry presentations begin.

Now, let's take a look at each of these recommendations in detail.

Recommendation One: Reach Out to Community Members About the Grammar Inquiry Presentations

An initial step of creating opportunities for students to share their grammar inquiry findings is to reach out to community members about the presentation events. To do this, I recommend first creating a flyer that describes the event. The flyer depicted in Figure 5.1 that I used for my seventh-graders' strong verb presentations provides one model of what such a document can look like. When constructing your own flyers, I recommend including the following information: 1) A title for the event (such as "Strong Verb Grammar Inquiry Presentations"), 2) The essential question that guided the students' work, 3) Information that describes what the students have done and will present, and 4) Catchy and friendly language that invites the flyer recipient to attend.

Once you've created a flyer that contains key information about the grammar inquiry presentations, the next step is sharing it with community members! As I mentioned earlier in this chapter, I shared the flyer for my students' grammar inquiry presentation with school administrators, other English teachers, and students' caregivers, while also giving copies to students for them to distribute to any individuals in their communities and out-of-school lives they would like, such as sports coaches, mentors, and anyone else that they want to invite. When sharing the flyer with school colleagues and students' caregivers, I send it attached to an email that provides additional information about the work students have done on the project. Similarly, when I give a copy of the flyer to students to distribute to important people in their lives, I share with them some context and background about the grammar inquiry project that they can include to give their guest more information about the work the students have done and what they've learned. This additional context provides the audience with information that conveys the important academic concepts students have engaged with, further emphasizing its significance.

Recommendation Two: Emphasize to Students That Grammar Inquiry Presentations are Opportunities to Share Real-World Ideas with Authentic Audiences

Before students present their grammar inquiries, I suggest emphasizing to them the authentic and relevant nature of their work. To do this, I recommend talking with students about how their grammar inquiry presentations are opportunities to share real-world ideas with authentic audiences. When I have these conversations with students, I remind them that a key aspect of grammar inquiries is that, in these inquiries, the students find examples of the focal concept in the authentic language use they encounter in their out-of-school lives. I then emphasize that one of the main goals of their grammar inquiries is for students to be able to understand the importance of that concept to authentic communication they find outside of school in their everyday lives.

Once I've discussed this information with students, I point out to them that their grammar inquiry presentations not only highlight real-world ideas and examples of language, but also are opportunities to share this information with authentic audiences (such as other students and adults in the school, caregivers, and any other community members they invite, as discussed in the preceding recommendation). For example, I emphasized both of these to my seventh graders as they prepared for their inquiry presentations, first highlighting the fact that "These strong verb grammar inquiries are based on language use in real life. They're all about the texts you find outside of school and why strong verbs are important to them." I then continued to highlight the authentic audience to which students would present: When you share your inquiries, you're not just going to be talking about real-world examples of strong verbs; you're also going to be sharing with a real-world audience of other students, community members, caregivers, and other people who go beyond just this classroom.

I closed by emphasizing the authentic nature of this work and providing encouragement: "You're sharing real-world ideas with a real-world audience, and I'm so excited to see the great work you'll do." I recommend highlighting these same kinds of authentic and real-world connections for your students before they share their inquiries.

Recommendation Three: Provide Students with Clear Guidelines For Their Grammar Inquiry Presentations

An important step for maximizing students' experiences on their grammar inquiry presentations is providing them with clear guidelines that explain what they need to do in order to be successful. By sharing this information with students, we will equip them with strong understandings of what their presentations should contain and address. I found these clear guidelines to be especially significant for this assignment because the grammar inquiry project is so different from the previous work my students had previously done with grammar. Since my students were engaging with grammatical concepts in such a different way in this project than they had before, the concrete guidelines I shared with them helped them understand exactly what to do in order to present their work successfully.

The example guidelines depicted in Figure 5.2 earlier in this chapter, which I shared with my tenth graders before they shared their subordinate clause inquiry presentations, provide a model for what these guidelines can look like. When you share presentation guidelines with your students, I recommend identifying the following information: 1) The presentation length, 2) Specific content you want the students to address (such as the essential question, an identification of an authentic use of the grammatical concept, and the students' analysis of that authentic example), and 3) Any other suggestions you think would help students succeed (for example, I asked students to include slides that contain text and images and to incorporate a concluding section that connects the identification and analysis with the essential question). I encourage you to consider the length of time you want students to present, content you want the students to be sure to include, and other suggestions and information you feel would help them be successful on these presentations. By sharing these ideas, you will provide students with guidelines that will facilitate their success in this work.

Recommendation Four: Purposefully Address Guests and Students before Grammar Inquiry Presentations Begin

This final recommendation highlights the importance of purposefully addressing guests and students before the grammar inquiry presentations begin. Prior to students presenting their inquiry findings, I suggest talking with both of these groups in purposeful ways that call attention to the meaningful and relevant work that students have done in this project. At the beginning of the presentation time, I first address the audience, welcoming them and sharing with them key information about the work students have done on this project. For example, when I welcomed the audience members who came to my seventh-graders' grammar inquiry presentations, I commended the students' hard work and then described the essential question. After that, I explained that students would be sharing strong verb identifications and analyses that align with their investigation of the essential question. Similarly, when you address and welcome the guests who attend your students' grammar inquiry presentations, I recommend discussing the essential question that students investigated and sharing with the audience that students will be describing identifications and analyses of the focal concept from their authentic experiences with language.

After welcoming and orienting the audience, I suggest also having a brief motivational talk with your students before they give their inquiry presentations. During these talks, I emphasize to students that I am proud of them for the great work they've done, identifying specific strengths and positive features that are specific to their work. For example, I have praised students for their hard work on a project, for the ways they've explored a variety of texts in their inquiries, and for their thoughtful analyses about the significance of the grammatical concept examples they found. I keep these talks concise and positive, and I end with a closing statement that sends them off to give their presentations with supportive energy. When having these brief pre-presentation talks with students, I suggest praising them for something specific about their grammar inquiry work that has impressed you, such as the ways they identified real-world examples of grammatical concepts, the analyses they created, or their responses to the essential question. After sharing this praise, I recommend concluding with an encouraging statement that expresses your confidence in their ability to do great work on their presentations or your excitement in seeing the work they will share. These talks can help encourage students and remind them of what they have accomplished before they share their inquiries.

Key Takeaway Points

This section identifies key takeaway points to consider as you engage in the meaningful work of creating opportunities for students to share their grammar inquiry findings.

- Students can share the findings of their grammar inquiries by giving presentations that describe the following information:
  - Their responses to the inquiry's essential question.
  - The authentic example of the focal grammatical concept they identified.
  - Their analysis of the importance of that grammatical concept to the text in which it was used.
- There are two especially significant aspects of constructing these opportunities for students:
  - Organizing community events where students will share the results of their inquiries.
  - Providing students with clear guidelines for sharing their findings.
- Creating opportunities for students to share their grammar inquiry findings is an especially significant aspect of this process and of students' experiences with it. There are three reasons why the action of students presenting their findings in the ways described in this chapter is especially important:
  - It makes the grammar inquiry experience meaningful for students.
  - It is motivational for them.
  - It is aligned with the values of grammar inquiries.

80 ◆ Opportunities for Students to Share Their Findings

- ◆ When creating opportunities for your students to share their grammar inquiry findings, I suggest using these instructional recommendations to inform your work:
  - Reach out to community members about the grammar inquiry presentations.
  - Emphasize to students that grammar inquiry presentations are opportunities to share real-world ideas with authentic audiences.
  - Provide students with clear guidelines for their grammar inquiry presentations.
  - Purposefully address guests and students before grammar inquiry presentations begin.
- ◆ The infographic in Figure 5.5 depicts these instructional recommendations.

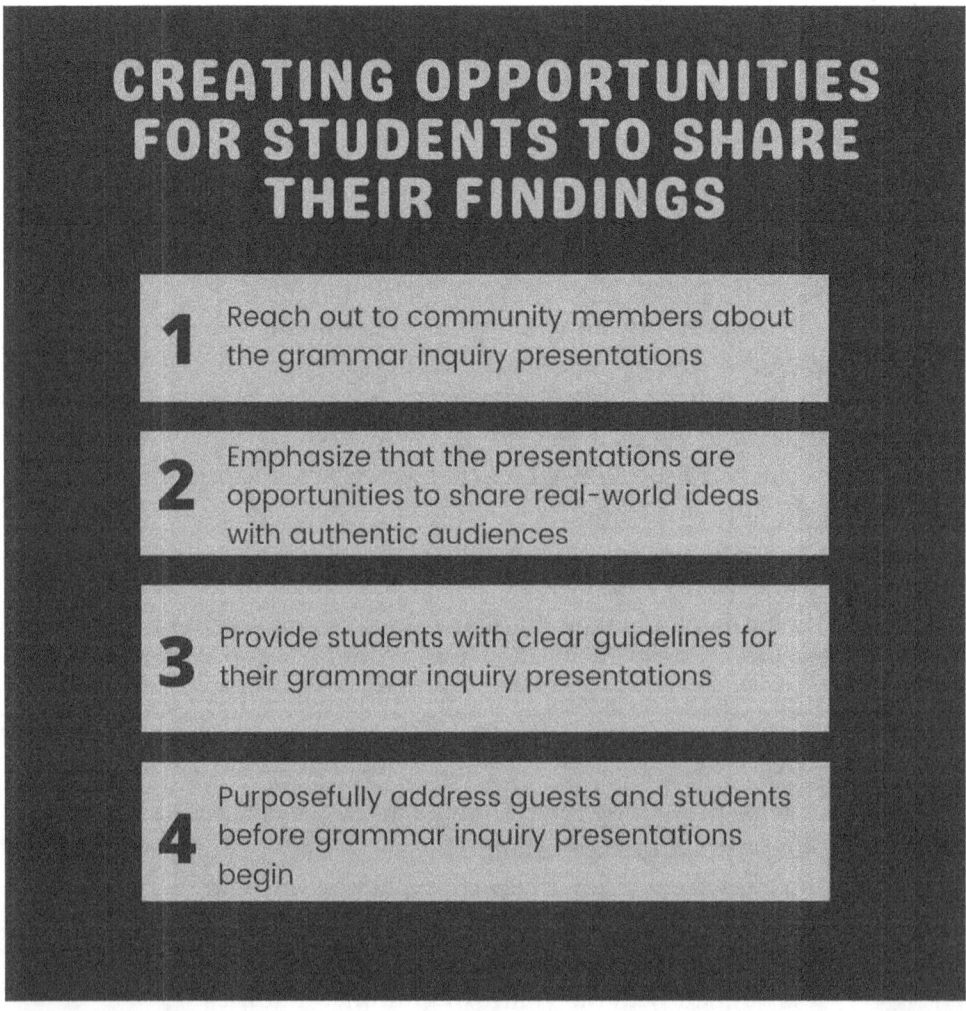

Figure 5.5 Infographic—Creating Opportunities for Students to Share Their Findings

6
Asking Students to Reflect on Their Experiences

In this chapter, we'll explore an important next step in students' work with inquiry-based grammar instruction: asking students to reflect on their experiences in this project and supporting them as they engage in this reflection. The chapter will provide you with information, explanations, examples, and suggestions to use as you ask your students to reflect on their grammar inquiry experiences and provide them with the support they need while they do so. Reflecting on their grammar inquiry experiences builds on the work that students have done throughout this project and helps them think metacognitively about what they've learned (Flavell, 1979), why that knowledge is important (Garner, 1987), and how it can impact their understanding of grammar (Ruday, 2020c). As we'll see in this chapter, these reflective experiences and the deep thinking skills they facilitate are great ways for students to think carefully about what they've learned in the grammar inquiry project and why that knowledge is important.

The chapter begins with information about what it means to ask students to reflect on their experiences with the grammar inquiry project, identifying key reflection prompts for students to consider and discussing ways to help students engage with them. After that, it discusses why students' reflecting on their grammar inquiry work is so important to their understanding of the authentic uses of grammatical concepts and of the significance of grammar to effective communication. Next, the chapter shares examples of students' reflections on their grammar inquiry experiences and discusses what we can learn from their reflective insights. After that, it provides instructional recommendations to use when helping your students reflect on their grammar

DOI: 10.4324/9781003424260-7

inquiries. It then concludes with key closing ideas and an infographic that expresses important instructional insights. Let's now explore the idea of students' reflecting on their grammar inquiry experiences.

What Is It?

At this point in the grammar inquiry process, students have considered their essential question, identified real-world examples of the focal concept, analyzed those examples, and presented their insights. However, there is still a very important part of their work remaining: reflecting on what they've learned in their grammar inquiries and why that knowledge is important. When students reflect on their grammar inquiry experiences, I ask them to craft written responses to two related reflection questions: 1) What did you learn about the focal concept by identifying and analyzing real-world examples of it? and 2) Why is what you learned in the grammar inquiry project important?

To make these questions even more concrete for students, I recommend inserting the specific grammatical concept you've studied, such as strong verbs, subordinate clauses, or any other topic into the question. For example, you could write "What did you learn about the focal concept of strong verbs by identifying and analyzing real world examples of it?" Before students begin their reflection experiences, I preview the activity, telling them that, while they've recently presented their grammar inquiry findings, there is one last step to their inquiry work. I then say that they will be reflecting on their grammar inquiry experiences by responding to questions about what they've learned and why that knowledge is important. Now, let's look closely at each of these reflection questions.

Reflection Question One: What Did You Learn About the Focal Concept by Identifying and Analyzing Real-World Examples of It?

Early on in students' reflection experiences, I introduce to them the question "What did you learn about the focal concept by identifying and analyzing real-world examples of it?" Before I ask students to write responses to the question, I ask them to take a few minutes to brainstorm ideas about what they learned and how they know that they've learned that information. For example, I told my seventh graders, Before you write an answer to this question, I want you to take a few minutes to write down some things that you've learned about strong verbs from our grammar inquiries. This can be something you learned from identifying real-world examples of strong verbs, something you learned from analyzing those examples by thinking about why they were used and how a text may have been different without them, or it can be something else you feel like you learned.

As students brainstorm this information, I circulate the room and check in with them, asking clarifying questions and noting especially strong student responses.

Reflection Question Two: Why is What You Learned in the Grammar Inquiry Project Important?

Next, I introduce students to the second reflection question that they'll answer as part of their grammar inquiry reflection experiences: "Why is what you learned in the grammar inquiry project important?" When I shared this question with my seventh graders, I explained that this question builds off of the first one, but also asks them to think differently about the topic: "The first question you'll respond to asks you what you learned," I told them. "This question is the next step: it asks you to reflect on why what you learned is important." I then explained to students that there are a variety of reasons the knowledge they learned can be important: This information could be important because it helped you understand strong verbs better, because it helped you understand how strong verbs are used in our everyday lives in so many ways, because it helped you understand the texts you investigated in your inquiry, or any other reason.

As with the first question, I ask students to brainstorm some possible ideas, this time about why what they learned in the grammar inquiry is important and why they think so. I again move around the room to monitor students' progress on the ideas they're brainstorming, providing any needed support and encouragement and identifying particularly insightful reflective statements.

Why Is It Important?

Students' reflections on their grammar inquiry project work are significant aspects of their learning experiences. By engaging in this reflective work, students develop the ability to recognize what they've learned and to build on the skills they've developed through their learning experiences (Helyer, 2015). Opportunities to reflect on what they've learned and why that information is important helps students engage in in-depth learning that they may not achieve without the chance and encouragement to reflect (Chang, 2019). Through these opportunities to reflect on their grammar inquiry work, students can develop a critical consciousness (Ladson-Billings, 1995) about grammar instruction by thinking carefully about the value of engaging with authentic examples of grammatical concepts and how doing so emphasizes the significance of these concepts to their real-world experiences with language. This reflective work is especially meaningful to students' grammar inquiry experiences for two key reasons: 1) Reflection encourages students to think deeply about what they've learned about real-world uses of grammatical concepts, and 2) Reflection helps students understand the importance of grammatical concepts to authentic communication. In this section, we'll explore each of these ideas.

Reflection Encourages Students to Think Deeply About What They've Learned About Real-World Uses of Grammatical Concepts

One key reason that students' reflections on their grammar inquiry experiences are important is that this reflective work encourages them to think deeply about what they've learned regarding the real-world uses of grammatical concepts. Grammar inquiries and their corresponding essential questions are designed to create opportunities for students to identify and analyze grammatical concepts they encounter in their everyday lives; when students take time and reflect on what they've learned about these grammatical concepts, they can deepen the knowledge they've gained in their inquiries. For example, when students reflect on what they learned about their focal concept by identifying and analyzing real-world examples of it, they think more in even more depth about the knowledge they developed through their work. While students certainly learn a great deal from the identifications and analyses they conduct in their grammar inquiries, that knowledge can become even deeper and more developed when they return to those inquiries and think further about what knowledge they gained from that work. Students can share their increased understandings of the features of the concept, the wide range of ways it is used, the role of that concept in their everyday communication, or anything else they've learned from the experience. All of these insights can help students think more deeply about their work.

Reflection Helps Students Understand the Importance of Grammatical Concepts to Authentic Communication

In addition to deepening the knowledge they've developed in their grammar inquiries, reflection can also help students understand the importance of grammatical concepts to authentic communication. When students take time following their inquiry work to think carefully about the real-world examples of grammatical concepts they've identified and analyzed, they can consider the meaningful role that those concepts have in all forms of communication, not just texts that are traditionally featured in school. Since grammar inquiries center students' authentic, real-world language experiences and the ways focal grammatical concepts figure in those experiences, students can use reflection opportunities to think about how the focal concepts are used in—and are important to—authentic texts they encounter outside of school. The reflection question "Why is what you learned in the grammar inquiry project important?" relates to this important benefit—it creates an opportunity for students to think about the essential question they investigated, the authentic examples they found, and how that information helped them develop their ideas about the significance of grammatical concepts to the language we encounter in real-world settings.

How Can It Look in Action?

In this section, we'll look at examples of students' reflections on their grammar inquiry experiences and then explore what we can learn from these reflective insights. First, we'll take a look at a reflection written by the student in my seventh-grade class whose insights on the strong verb "devoured" in a conversation about a dog's eating habits were featured in Chapters 4 and 5. An excerpt from this student's reflection is depicted in Figure 6.1. The excerpt is part of the student's response to the question "What did you learn about the focal concept of strong verbs by identifying and analyzing real world examples of it?"

Grade Seven Student Reflection Example: Strong Verbs

> I learned a whole lot about strong verbs by identifying and analyzing real world examples. One of the big things I learned is that strong verbs really are everywhere. I picked the strong verb "devoured" from when my brother was talking with me about how our dog ate his food, but, once I identified that one, I also noticed a bunch more. When I really started thinking about strong verbs, it was like I could find them everywhere! I also learned a lot about how strong verbs are a really big deal to saying what you want to say. What I mean by that is that strong verbs really help you say something exactly the way you want. I learned this really well when I was analyzing the importance of the strong verb "devoured." Doing this really showed me that strong verbs help you say something the way you want to say it. If you don't use a strong verb and use a weaker one–like "ate" instead of "devoured"--you wouldn't be able to say what you want to say the exact way you want. I learned that strong verbs are everywhere and are super important to saying what you want to say!

Figure 6.1 Strong Verb Reflection Example

What We Can Learn From It

This student's reflection shows the awareness he developed about the prevalence of strong verbs in all forms of communication, as exhibited through his statement "One of the big things I learned is that strong verbs really are everywhere." In addition, his reflection conveys his understanding of the role that strong verbs can play in effective communication, which he demonstrates through the observation that "…strong verbs really help you say something the way you want to say it." These reflective insights represent the meaningful learning and thinking he did about strong verbs as a result of the grammar inquiry project. The student's thoughtful insights show that he used this activity as an opportunity to engage in meaningful reflection about what he learned about strong verbs and how the understandings he developed are personally meaningful to him.

Now, let's take a look at a reflection excerpt from the student in my tenth-grade class. This student's identification and analysis of a subordinate clause

Grade Ten Student Reflection Example: Subordinate Clauses

> Why is what I learned in the grammar inquiry project important?
>
> I think what I learned in the grammar inquiry project is important because it took grammar beyond the way I learned it before in school and helped me understand it a lot more. In school before, grammar was always worksheets, and teachers correcting my work, and those things where the teacher gives you something with errors in it and you find the errors. It was all about correcting things. What I learned in the grammar inquiry project is that grammar isn't just about correcting things. It can be about finding grammar, like subordinate clauses, in your real-world communication, like the text message where I found my example. This made grammar more interesting and relevant to my life, but it also helped me understand it a lot more. I thought about subordinate clauses much more in the grammar inquiry project than I would have with worksheets and correcting things. When I gave my presentation last week, I said that the subordinate clause I used was important because if I didn't use it, my friends wouldn't have known why I was offering fries. I definitely never thought about grammar in this much depth before. What I learned in the grammar inquiry project is important because the project showed me that grammar is a part of real-world communication and because it helped me understand grammar more than I did before.

Figure 6.2 Subordinate Clause Reflection Example

in a text message to his friends about buying french fries with a gift card to Five Guys restaurant was highlighted in Chapters Four and Five. An excerpt from this student's response is depicted in Figure 6.2. It is part of the student's response to the question "Why is what you learned in the grammar inquiry project important?"

What We Can Learn From It

From this student's reflection, we can see how the grammar inquiry project can provide students with relevant and meaningful experiences with grammar instruction that also deepen their abilities to think about the significance of grammatical concepts. An especially important aspect of this student's reflective work is the statement "This made grammar more interesting and relevant to my life, but it also helped me understand it a lot more." In this observation and the others associated with it, the student relates that the real-world connections facilitated by the grammar inquiry project led to both increased engagement and deeper learning. These reflections emphasize the valuable learning experiences that can come from asset-based grammar instruction that, as discussed in the book's introduction, prioritizes the application of knowledge to students' authentic communication instead of deficit based-instruction that focuses primarily on factual recall without real-world connections or applications. By reflecting on these ideas, this student shared important aspects of his experience. In addition, through his reflective insights, he was able to further process his thoughts about why the grammar inquiry project was meaningful to him.

Instructional Recommendations

Now, let's look together at four key instructional recommendations to consider and utilize as you help your students reflect on their grammar inquiry project experiences. The instructional suggestions described here are:

1. Preview the reflective activity, explaining what it is and why it matters.
2. Introduce students to the reflection questions and create brainstorming opportunities.
3. Share reflection guidelines with students.
4. Model some of your own reflective insights.

Let's explore each of these suggestions individually.

Recommendation One: Preview the Reflective Activity, Explaining What It Is and Why It Matters

I recommend first providing students with a brief preview of the reflective work they will do in this activity by explaining what they will be doing and why doing so is important. I have found that sharing this initial information with students creates a foundation for their experiences that ultimately helps them be successful. When I preview the reflective work with students, I tell them there is one last step to what they've done on the grammar inquiry project, and introduce them to what they'll do in this final stage. For example, when introducing this reflective work to my tenth graders, I told them

> The last thing you'll do for this grammar inquiry on subordinate clauses is to reflect on your experience by answering some questions about your experiences in the grammar inquiry project. These reflection questions will ask you to think about what you learned in the grammar inquiry project and why what you learned is important.

After this, I talked with the students about why this reflective work matters:

> I'm asking you to answer these reflection questions because reflecting on this information can help enhance your learning even more. Research shows that reflecting on what we've learned and why it's important deepens our knowledge compared to if we didn't reflect. This will be a great concluding activity to our grammar inquiry work that will also deepen your knowledge about what you've learned in this process.

When you preview this reflective work for your students, I suggest following the same steps I used with my students. First, introduce the work to them by saying that they'll be reflecting on their grammar inquiries. Next, talk with the students about how reflection can deepen their learning and understanding. This information will provide students with a strong starting point and set them up for success in the rest of their reflective work.

Recommendation Two: Introduce Students To The Reflection Questions and Create Brainstorming Opportunities

Once you've previewed the reflective work for students by orienting them to the activities they'll be doing and their importance, the students can move forward in this process. To help students take the next step in their reflection, I suggest introducing them to the reflection questions to which they'll respond and create opportunities for them to brainstorm responses to those questions. As I shared in "What Is It?" section earlier in this chapter, I first introduce the students to the reflection question "What did you learn about the focal concept by identifying and analyzing real-world examples of it?" and then ask them to brainstorm some ideas about what they learned and how they know they learned that information. To help students conduct these brainstorms, it can be useful to share with them a graphic organizer to help them structure their ideas. Figure 6.3 contains the graphic organizer I shared with my students; it is also available in Appendix B. When I give the graphic organizer to students, I tell them that I know all people organize their thoughts differently and that there are a variety of ways to record one's thinking. I tell them that this is one way to express the ideas they have, but they can also brainstorm in other ways, such as making lists, freewriting, or using another way to record their thinking. The graphic organizer example I share with them lists the reflection question in the center and contains four circles connected to it in which to brainstorm some ideas. I explain to students that, if they use this graphic organizer, they don't have to fill in each circle and they can also draw more if they have additional ideas they want to share. I want them to feel like they have ownership of the document and they can use it in ways that will be most helpful to them. While students brainstorm their ideas, using this graphic organizer or another format, I check in with them to provide support, asking questions when relevant and praising strong responses.

After students have brainstormed their ideas about the first reflection question, I recommend sharing with them the second reflection question they'll consider: "Why is what you learned in the grammar inquiry project important?" As I shared in the "What Is It?" section earlier in this chapter, I like to talk with students about how this question is different from the first one they responded to, calling attention to the way that the first reflection question asks them what they learned while this one asks them to reflect on what that they learned was important. I suggest asking students to brainstorm possible ideas and responses related to this question by noting their thoughts about why what they learned in the grammar inquiry project is important and why they think so. Like with the first reflection question, I recommend providing students with a graphic organizer that they can use when brainstorming possible ideas, but also emphasizing that there are a variety of ways to record one's thoughts and that they are welcome to brainstorm in other ways if that works best for them. The graphic organizer I share with my students that relates to the second reflection question is depicted in Figure 6.4 and is also available in Appendix B. While students brainstorm, I recommend circulating the room to check in with them and provide feedback and support.

Recommendation Three: Share Reflection Guidelines with Students

The next step in preparing students to engage in strong and meaningful reflective work is sharing with them guidelines for their reflective responses. Like when students gave their grammar inquiry presentations, these guidelines

90 ◆ Asking Students to Reflect on Their Experiences

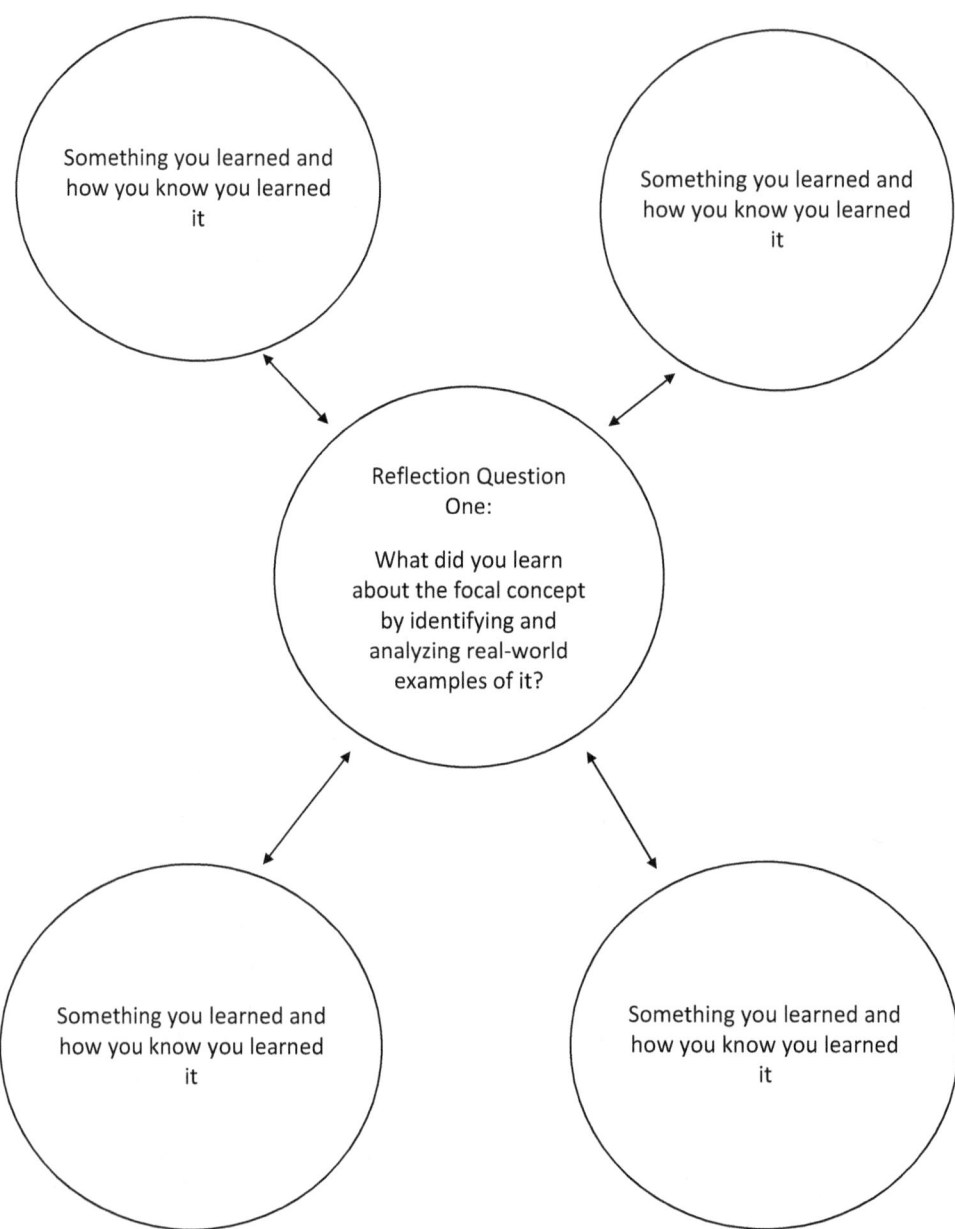

Figure 6.3 Reflection Question One Brainstorm Template

provide students with clear understandings of what they'll do in their reflection responses. While guidelines in general are helpful and important for students, I found that my students especially appreciated the reflection guidelines I shared with them because a number of them had not done similar reflective work and were unsure of what to do. The student in my seventh-grade class whose strong verb insights are featured in this book shared with me "I was glad you gave us guidelines about what to do in the reflection. That

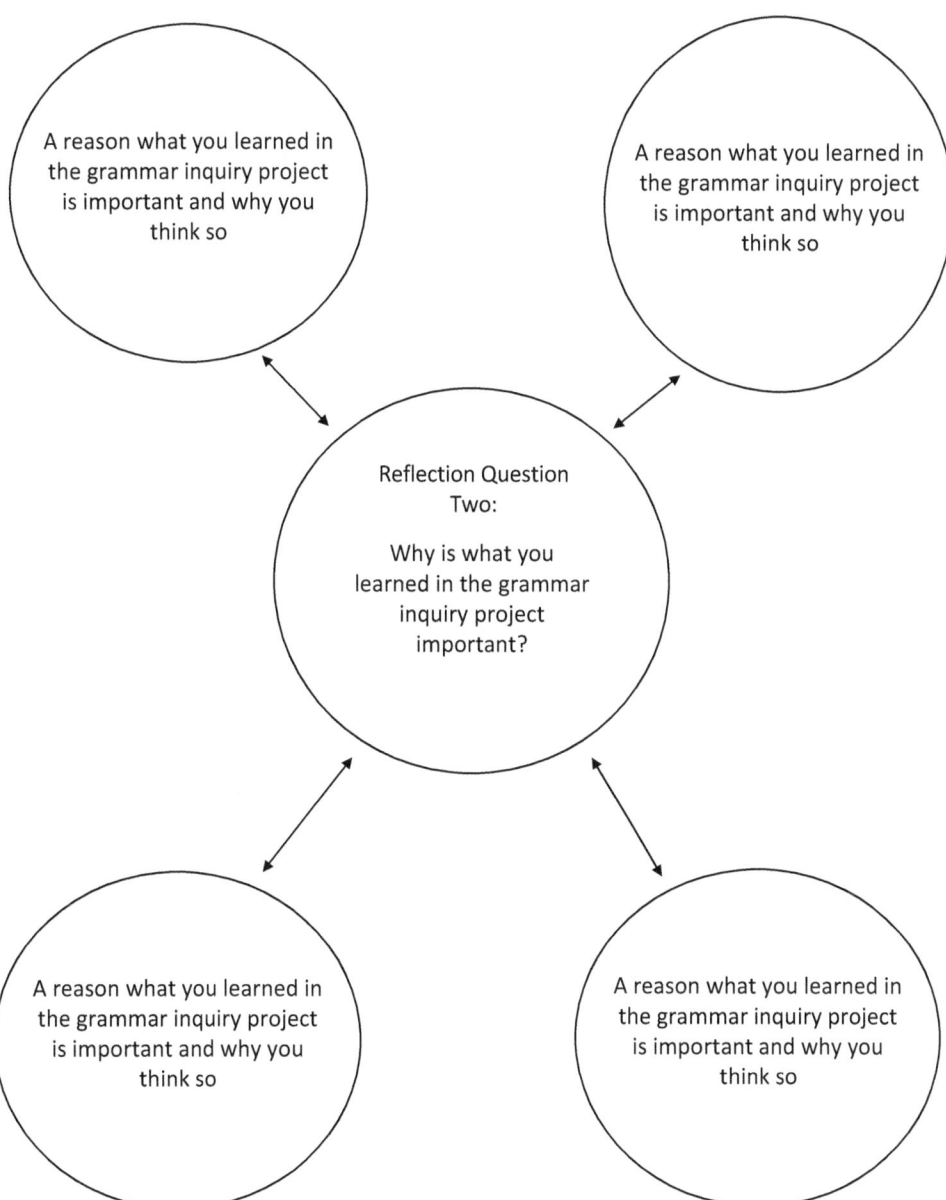

Figure 6.4 Reflection Question Two Brainstorm Template

made it a lot easier for me to understand how to write a reflection." Figure 6.5 contains the reflection guidelines I shared with seventh graders.

When you create reflection guidelines to share with your students, I recommend following a similar format to the example I shared with my students. First, I suggest reminding students of the work they did on their inquiries to emphasize the connection between that work and this reflective activity. Next, I like to provide students with the reflection questions so they will have

> **Strong Verb Reflection Guidelines!**
>
> Wonderful job on all of your work on our grammar inquiry project! You all have done such great work thinking carefully about our essential question "How do strong verbs make the texts we encounter outside of school as effective as possible?," identifying examples of strong verbs, and analyzing the importance of those examples. I am so proud of all of you!
>
> The final step in our grammar inquiry work is to write a reflection on your learning. As we have discussed, in this reflection you will answer two questions: "What did you learn about the focal concept of strong verbs by identifying and analyzing real world examples of it?" and "Why is what you learned in the grammar inquiry project important?"
>
> Here are some guidelines that will help you as you write your reflections:
> - Your answer to each question should be around one paragraph long.
> - Your answer to each question should reveal your own thoughtful ideas and careful reflections regarding that question.
> - The ideas in your answers should be supported by specific examples and details from your own grammar inquiries, such as an example you identified and your analysis of that example.
> - These answers are specific to you, so there is no "right" or "wrong" response. I am looking for your ideas about each reflection question and specific examples that support the ideas you share.
> - Feel free to use any of our in-class brainstorms to help you while you write.
>
> Just let me know if you have any questions! I am excited to read your reflections!

Figure 6.5 Reflection Guidelines Example

clear understandings of what they're discussing. After that, I recommend providing a list of key guidelines that identify a suggested length for their responses and emphasize that the reflections should contain students' own insights with support from specific examples from their inquiry work. These details can help students understand what their guidelines should look like, equipping them with key information that will help them succeed on this important work.

Recommendation Four: Model Some of Your Own Reflective Insights

As a final step in preparing students to reflect on their grammar inquiry experiences, I recommend sharing some of your reflections on your own grammar inquiry work. To do so, I suggest first returning to the examples of authentically used grammatical concepts from your own authentic communication that you shared with students earlier in the instructional activities described in this book, such as the identification of a real-world grammatical concept from your own life discussed in Chapter Two and the corresponding analysis in Chapter Three. Next, I recommend talking with students about how you would answer each of the two reflection questions based on the work you did identifying and analyzing these examples. When I do this, I review with students the authentic examples of the focal concept that I identified and analyzed and the share slides that contain ideas I would share in my reflections on this work.

For example, before my tenth graders wrote their reflections on their subordinate clause grammar inquiries, I told them that I was going to share my own reflections: Remember the examples of subordinate clauses from my own authentic communication that I shared with you? They were from a conversation I had with a friend about running a road race. One of them was "Since the first two miles are all uphill, I suggest starting the race at an easy pace." In this sentence, I used the subordinate clause "Since the first two miles are all uphill." The other was "I love the middle part of the race because there is a big, cheering crowd there," which contains the subordinate clause "because there is a big, cheering crowd there."

After I reminded students of these examples, I shared slides that contained highlights of responses to the reflections I would share. I first presented a slide that contained the reflection question "What did you learn about the focal concept of subordinate clauses by identifying and analyzing real-world examples of it?" and some of my reflections on that topic: I learned that I use subordinate clauses so much in my everyday communication and that the information they provide is extremely important to the effectiveness of that communication. The examples I shared about running are good representations of this because the information in them plays such a big role in the message I shared with my audience.

I then displayed a new slide that contained the second reflection question "Why is what you learned in the grammar inquiry project important?" On this slide, I also shared the text:

What I learned in my grammar inquiry is important because it emphasized to me that grammar is a tool that we use in everyday communication to share ideas effectively and clearly. I think it's so important to see grammar like this so that we can really understand how grammar concepts like subordinate clauses are meaningful to everyday communication.

Sharing reflection excerpts like these can give your students a starting point as they begin to engage in their own reflective work.

Key Takeaway Points

This section contains important takeaway ideas that will help you as you ask students to reflect on their grammar inquiry experiences and support them as they do so.

- At this stage in the grammar inquiry process, students reflect on what they've learned in their grammar inquiries and why that knowledge is important.
- When students reflect on their grammar inquiry experiences, I ask them to craft written responses to two related reflection questions:
  - What did you learn about the focal concept by identifying and analyzing real-world examples of it?
  - Why is what you learned in the grammar inquiry project important?
- Students' reflections on their grammar inquiry project work are especially important to their experiences for two key reasons:
  - Reflection encourages students to think deeply about what they've learned about real-world uses of grammatical concepts.
  - Reflection helps students understand the importance of grammatical concepts to authentic communication.
- When asking students to reflect on their grammar inquiry project experiences and supporting them through this work, I recommend following these instructional suggestions:
  - Preview the reflective activity, explaining what it is and why it matters.
  - Introduce students to the reflection questions and create brainstorming opportunities.
  - Share reflection guidelines with students.
- Model some of your own reflective insights.
- The infographic in Figure 6.6 depicts these instructional recommendations.

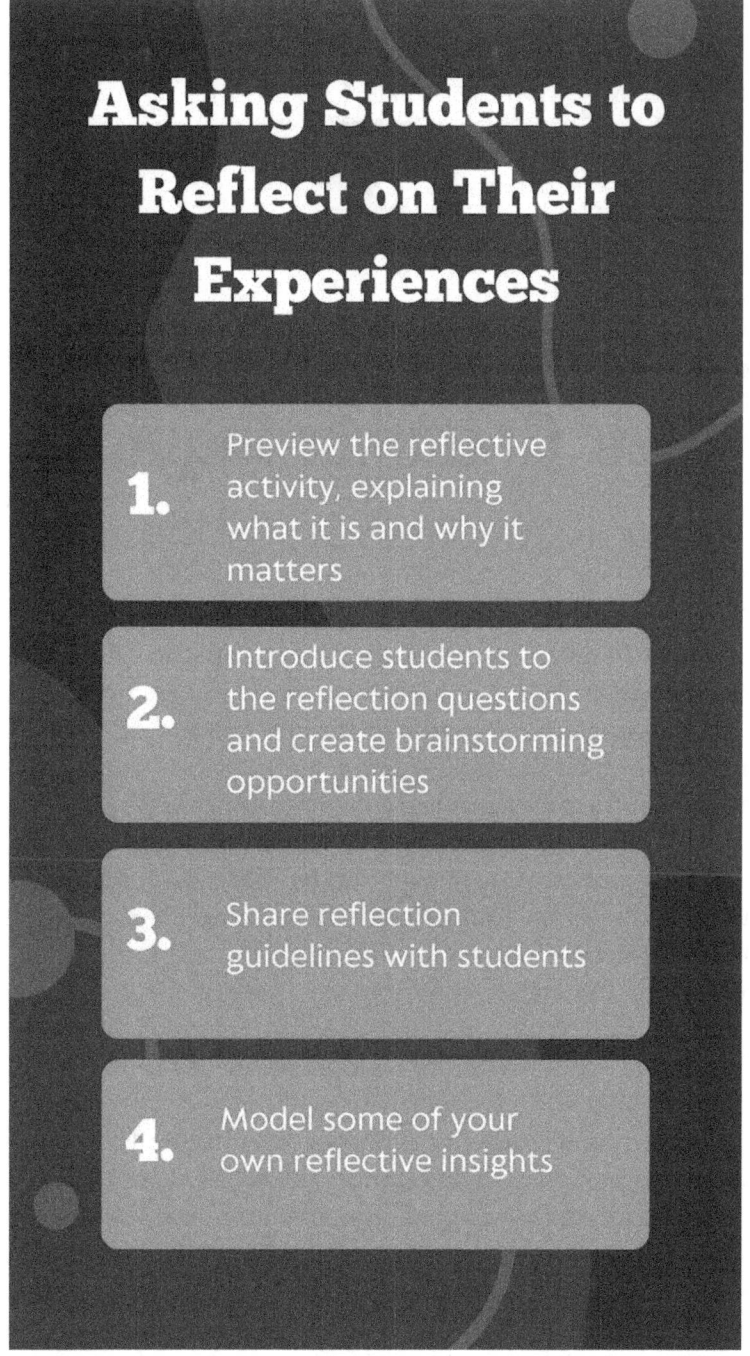

Figure 6.6 Infographic—Asking Students to Reflect on Their Experiences

7

Assessing Students' Work on Their Grammar Inquiries

In this chapter, we'll look together at another essential component of inquiry-based grammar instruction: assessing students' work on their grammar inquiries. At this stage in the grammar inquiry process, students have completed their work: they have considered the examples you've shared with them, identified authentic examples of the focal concept that is central to their inquiries, analyzed those examples, shared their findings with an audience, and written reflections on their experiences. The one remaining step is to assess students' work in a summative way and provide them feedback that will help them continue to grow for future grammar inquiries and for their future work with language and grammar in general. This chapter will provide you with important information and ideas that will help you assess your students' grammar inquiry work in meaningful ways.

The chapter begins with information about what it means to assess students' work on their grammar inquiries, identifying key components of these assessments, and sharing an example rubric. Next, it explores why effective and meaningful assessments of students' grammar inquiry work are so important to their learning experiences with this process. After that, it shares examples of how I used the rubric provided in this chapter to assess the work of the seventh- and tenth-grade students whose ideas and insights have been featured in this book. Following that, the chapter offers recommendations to consider as you evaluate your own students on their grammar inquiry work. Finally, it concludes with important final insights and a useful infographic that summarizes essential recommendations for your own assessment work. Now, let's begin our exploration of grammar inquiry assessment!

DOI: 10.4324/9781003424260-8

What Is It?

At this stage in the grammar inquiry process, we provide our students with a summative evaluation of their grammar inquiry presentations and reflections. In order to assess students' work on their grammar inquiry projects, it's important to identify key evaluation components and tools that will help us evaluate their performance and give them meaningful feedback that communicates their areas of strength and of future growth. In this section, we'll look at two key elements of grammar inquiry assessment as well as an example rubric, which I used when evaluating my seventh- and tenth-grade students on their grammar inquiries. First, we'll explore key ideas to keep in mind when evaluating students' grammar inquiry presentations. Next, we'll look at important ideas to consider when evaluating students' grammar inquiry reflections. Finally, I'll share and discuss the example rubric that I used when providing my students with a summative assessment on their grammar inquiry work.

Assessing Students' Grammar Inquiry Presentations

When I assess students' grammar inquiry presentations, I focus on the grammar inquiry presentation guidelines that I shared with students before they gave their presentations and use those guidelines to identify the key criteria on which I will assess the students' presentations. For example, here are the grammar inquiry guidelines that I shared with my tenth graders before they presented their inquiry results (these guidelines are also depicted in Figure 5.2):

- The presentation should be three to five minutes long.
- It should include slides that contain text and relevant images.
- The presentation content should relate to the grammar inquiry essential question: "Why are subordinate clauses important tools for communication in our everyday lives?"
- The presentation should identify an example of a subordinate clause you identified in your everyday life.
- In the presentation, you should analyze the importance of the subordinate clause you identified by discussing why the text's creator may have used the subordinate clause and how the text would be different if the subordinate clause was not used.
- The presentation should have a concluding section that connects your subordinate clause identification and analysis with the essential question.

All of these ideas inform the criteria that I use when I evaluate students' work on their presentations. I assess the work based on the length of the presentation, its use of textual and relevant visual components, the relevance of the presentation content to the essential question, the identification of an authentically used example of the focal concept, the analysis of the importance of that concept, and the concluding connection between the example the student has shared and the essential question. By assessing students on these attributes, I can effectively evaluate their work on meaningful components of their inquiry presentations.

Assessing Students' Grammar Inquiry Reflections

Similarly, when assessing students' reflections on their grammar inquiries, I use the grammar inquiry reflection guidelines that I previously shared with them to identify the criteria that I will use to evaluate their reflective work. In these reflections, students respond to the questions "What did you learn about the focal concept by identifying and analyzing real-world examples of it?" and "Why is what you learned in the grammar inquiry project important?" The reflection guidelines I gave my students before they wrote their grammar inquiry reflections are listed here (and are also available in Figure 6.5):

- Your answer to each question should be around one paragraph long.
- Your answer to each question should reveal your own thoughtful ideas and careful reflections regarding that question.
- The ideas in your answers should be supported by specific examples and details from your own grammar inquiries, such as an example you identified and your analysis of that example.
- These answers are specific to you, so there is no "right" or "wrong" response. I am looking for your ideas about each reflection question and specific examples that support the ideas you share.
- Feel free to use any of our in-class brainstorms to help you while you write.

When I create the criteria on which I'll assess students' reflections, I particularly draw on the first three of the guidelines. I evaluate the work based primarily on the way it conveys the students' ideas about each reflection question and the specific examples, details, and insights that correspond with those ideas. Evaluating students' reflections based on these components allows me to assess them in meaningful ways that align with the main goals of their reflective work and the guidelines I shared with them.

Example Assessment Rubric

Now, let's take a look at the rubric that I use to assess students' work on their grammar inquiry presentations and reflections. Since the presentations and reflections are both part of students' work on the grammar inquiry projection, I like to combine their assessments on these works into one rubric in order to give them an overall evaluation of their performance. When I assess students' grammar inquiries, I use a single-point rubric (Fluckiger, 2010). This rubric format identifies the criteria for each rubric component and contains space for the teacher to record strengths and notes on areas for improvement for each of the criteria. When I use this rubric, I also provide a score between one and five for each category. At the end of the rubric, I share the total score from all of the categories and a concluding comment at the end of the rubric that identifies key strengths and areas of future growth regarding the student's work. I have found this to be a useful and easy-to-understand format for providing students with useful feedback. The rubric I have used when evaluating students' grammar inquiries is depicted in Figure 7.1 and is available in Appendix B.

Areas of Improvement	Criteria	Strengths
	The presentation is three to five minutes long and stays on topic throughout. Score:_____/5	
	The presentation slides include a combination of text and relevant images. Score:_____/5	
	The presentation content relates to the grammar inquiry's essential question. Score:_____/5	
	The presentation identifies an authentic example of the focal concept that the presenter found. Score:_____/5	

Figure 7.1 Grammar Inquiry Rubric

(Continued)

	The presentation contains a thoughtful analysis of the identified example that discusses why the text's creator may have used the focal concept and how the text would be different without it. Score: _____ /5	
	The presentation contains a concluding section that clearly connects the identification and analysis with the essential question Score: _____ /5	
	The answer to each reflection question is approximately one paragraph long and stays on topic throughout. Score: _____ /5	
	The answer to each question reveals thoughtful ideas and careful reflections regarding that question. Score: _____ /5	
	The ideas in the responses are supported by specific examples and details from the writer's own grammar inquiries. Score: _____ /5	

Total score: _____ /45

Percentage:

Comments:

Figure 7.1 (Continued)

Why Is It Important?

Assessing students' work on their grammar inquiries in thoughtful and detailed ways shows students that we value their authentic connections, communicates the strengths of what they've done, and expresses ways that they can continue to grow. The National Council of Teachers of English (NCTE) Position Statement on Assessment "Literacy Assessment: Definitions, Principles, and Practices" (2018) lists among its "Principles of Literacy Assessment" that "Literacy assessment is meaningful to the learner" (para. 5) and "Literacy assessments…help stakeholders focus on strengths, areas of concerns, goals for improvement, and actions to be taken" (para. 4). The assessment rubric discussed in this chapter incorporates these principles: it provides meaningful feedback to students about the authentic and relevant work they did in their inquiries that identifies what they have done well and ways they can continue to grow. In this section, we'll explore three key reasons why the summative grammar inquiry assessment practice discussed in this chapter is important: it shows students that we value their work, it communicates the strengths of their presentations and reflections, and it indicates how they can continue to develop. We'll take a look at each of these ideas individually.

It Shows Students That We Value Their Work

Providing students with detailed feedback and informative comments on their grammar inquiry presentations and reflections indicates that we value their work and effort they put into it. By identifying the strengths of their grammar inquiries and making suggestions for improvement that they can apply to other grammar inquiries and to their overall work on grammar, language, and literacy, we show students that we recognize and value what they've done. In contrast, if we did not provide students with detailed feedback and informative comments on their grammar inquiry work, our assessment practices would not express the same level of value and recognition for students' works. This recognition of students' work is especially important given the authentic connections to students' cultures and out-of-school lives that are part of the grammar inquiry process. Since students' grammar inquiries can represent their communities, cultures, and lived experiences, it is especially important that we value their work: doing so makes clear that we value the connections to students' cultures, identities, and communities that they share.

It Communicates the Strengths of Their Presentations and Reflections

Another important component of detailed and informative summative assessments of students' grammar inquiry work is that these evaluations communicate to students the strengths of their presentations and reflections. By sharing with students specific information about the presentations they gave and the reflections they wrote, we can let them know what aspects of their identifications, analyses, essential question connections, and reflections were especially strong and representative of excellent work. These positive comments not only validate students' work and acknowledge their strong performances, but also raise their awareness of particular aspects of their literacy skills that are particularly strong. For example, if we communicate to a student that they showed a great ability to reflect carefully on the importance of a grammatical concept or demonstrated strong reflection skills, we help them develop their awareness of these skills. Fletcher and Portalupi (2001) call for teachers to build on students' strengths when giving them feedback on their work in order to help them develop knowledge and confidence regarding their literacy abilities. Detailed feedback that identifies students' strengths helps achieve this goal.

It Indicates How Students Can Continue to Develop

In addition, the feedback that students receive on their grammar inquiry assessments shows them how they can continue to develop and grow in their literacy work. This feature aligns with the NCTE Position Statement on Assessment's (2018) assertion that effective literacy assessments identify "…areas of concerns, goals for improvement, and actions to be taken" (para. 4). When we share comments in the "Areas of Improvement" section of the grammar inquiry assessment rubric, we provide students with concrete statements about ways they can further maximize the strength of their work. For example, in the section of the rubric that reads "The presentation content relates to the grammar inquiry's essential question," we might (if applicable) note ways that the information in a student's grammar inquiry presentation could be even more clear and directly connected with the essential question of their inquiry. The suggestions for improvement we give students on their grammar inquiries are applicable to their future grammar inquiry work, but also can be applied to other work they do in English, literacy, and sometimes other subject areas as well. For instance, if we tell a student that their reflection could benefit from additional examples and details to support its central idea, the student could apply this feedback to not only other grammar inquiry reflections, but also other pieces they write that involve the use of details to support a key idea or argument. The specific feedback we give students on their grammar inquiry assessments can facilitate this growth.

How Can It Look In Action?

In this section, I share examples of how I used the grammar inquiry rubric in Figure 7.1 to assess and comment on the seventh- and tenth-grade students whose work has been featured in this book. Let's take a look at each of these rubrics and discuss what we can learn from them.

Seventh-Grade Assessment Example

First, we'll look together at the completed rubric that I used when assessing the strong verb grammar inquiry of the seventh-grade student whose work on the topic has been discussed in this book. As part of his investigation of the essential question "How do strong verbs make the texts we encounter outside of school as effective as possible?," this student identified and analyzed the strong verb "devoured" in his grammar inquiry. Figure 7.2 depicts the rubric with comments on and assessment of his work.

    The comments and scores on this rubric communicate the many strengths of the work that he did on his strong verb grammar inquiry, such as the excellent strong verb example he identified, the thoughtful insights he shared when explaining how his work on the grammar inquiry helped him understand the essential question, and the strong insights he shared in the reflection about how "strong verbs really are everywhere." The rubric and comments also provide this student with ideas he can use to strengthen his future work on grammar inquiry presentations, such as incorporating visuals in slides and pausing between explanations to help the audience process key information.

Tenth-Grade Assessment Example

Now, let's look at a rubric containing my assessment of the subordinate clause grammar inquiry of the tenth-grade student whose work has been featured in this book. This student investigated the essential question "Why are subordinate clauses important tools for communication in our everyday lives?" He identified and analyzed the subordinate clause "Since I got a Five Guys gift card" that he used in a text message to his friends. Figure 7.3 depicts the rubric containing an assessment of his work.

    The feedback on this student's rubric identifies and discusses the many significant strengths of his work, such as the focused and visually appealing presentation, the thoughtful connections to the essential questions, the insightful analysis of the importance of the subordinate clause to the student's work, and the thoughtful way the student reflected on the impact of his experience with this project. The information on the rubric and in the follow-up comment

Areas of Improvement	Criteria	Strengths
The presentation was a bit quick; next time, take time to pause between explanations to let the audience process the information.	The presentation is three to five minutes long and stays on topic throughout. Score: 4/5	You stayed on topic very well!
The slides would be stronger and more engaging with additional visual images.	The presentation slides include a combination of text and relevant images. Score: 3/5	The text in your slides was relevant and important!
	The presentation content relates to the grammar inquiry's essential question. Score: 5/5	Great job of clearly connecting the presentation content to the essential question.
	The presentation identifies an authentic example of the focal concept that the presenter found. Score: 5/5	Great work here. "Devoured" is an excellent strong verb example!
	The presentation contains a thoughtful analysis of the identified example that discusses why the text's creator may have used the focal concept and how the text would be different without it. Score: 5/5	You did an excellent job of discussing the importance of this strong verb to the conversation in which it was used. Great job!
	The presentation contains a concluding section that clearly connects the identification and analysis with the essential question. Score: 5/5	You did an especially impressive job of explaining how your work helped you understand the essential question!
	The answer to each reflection question is approximately one paragraph long and stays on topic throughout.	Your reflection question answers were full, informative paragraphs and are on-topic throughout.

Figure 7.2 Example Grammar Inquiry Rubric: Seventh Grade

(Continued)

	Score: 5/5	
	The answer to each question reveals thoughtful ideas and careful reflections regarding that question. Score: 5/5	Each of your reflection question answers showed your careful thinking. I especially appreciate your thoughtful statement "strong verbs really are everywhere."
	The ideas in the responses are supported by specific examples and details from the writer's own grammar inquiries. Score: 5/5	You did a great job here of drawing on details from your own inquiry, such as when you compared the strong verb "devour" to a weaker verb like "ate."

Total score: 42/45

Percentage: 93%

Comments:

You did an excellent job on your grammar inquiry work! You identified an excellent strong verb example in "devoured," which you picked from an authentic conversation about the way your dog ate his food. You analyzed this strong verb very well and did an outstanding job of connecting it to the essential question we studied. Your reflection was outstanding–it showed your careful thinking about the presence of strong verbs and drew on details from your inquiry very well. The only things that could have made the presentation even stronger were using even more visuals in the slides and pausing between some of the explanations to let the audience process important information, but this is still excellent work! Great job on this strong verb grammar inquiry!

Figure 7.2 (Continued)

shows the student specific ways that he excelled on this project, helping him be aware of these strengths of his work. This understanding of exactly what he did well on this grammar inquiry project can help the student succeed in similar ways in other grammar inquiries and on other literacy assignments in general.

Areas of Improvement	Criteria	Strengths
	The presentation is three to five minutes long and stays on topic throughout. Score: 5/5	Great job of delivering a focused presentation of just under five minutes.
	The presentation slides include a combination of text and relevant images. Score: 5/5	Excellent work on combining text and images. The images of Five Guys and of the french fries had visual appeal. You also used images to show the relationship between information. Nice job!
	The presentation content relates to the grammar inquiry's essential question. Score: 5/5	You made connections to the essential question throughout the presentation.
	The presentation identifies an authentic example of the focal concept that the presenter found. Score: 5/5	Yes, the example of the subordinate clause about the Five Guys gift card from a text message is an excellent authentic example.
	The presentation contains a thoughtful analysis of the identified example that discusses why the text's creator may have used the focal concept and how the text would be different without it. Score: 5/5	Great job of doing this. I appreciate your thoughtful statements about how the subordinate clause you used gave background information and explanation regarding the independent clause. I like how you said "Without the subordinate clause, they wouldn't know why I'm buying these fries for them."
	The presentation contains a concluding section that clearly connects the identification and analysis with the essential question. Score: 5/5	You made strong connections to this essential question at the end of the presentation (as well as at other points) that showed your ideas about why subordinate clauses are important tools for communication in our everyday lives.

Figure 7.3 Example Grammar Inquiry Rubric: Tenth Grade

(Continued)

	The answer to each reflection question is approximately one paragraph long and stays on topic throughout. Score: 5/5	Your reflection question responses were clearly connected to the topic and were each informative paragraphs.
	The answer to each question reveals thoughtful ideas and careful reflections regarding that question. Score: 5/5	Your answers to these questions very effectively revealed your reflections, such as your excellent point that the grammar inquiry project "took grammar beyond" the way you learned it in school and helped you understand it more.
	The ideas in the responses are supported by specific examples and details from the writer's own grammar inquiries. Score: 5/5	Wonderful job of using details from your own inquiry to make the reflection specific. Your reference to information you shared in your inquiry presentation about the importance of the subordinate clause you used provided useful detail here.

Total score: 45/45

Percentage: 100%

Comments:

Outstanding work on your grammar inquiry project! You excelled in every area of this project: you gave an informative, insightful, and engaging presentation that showed your strong understandings of why subordinate clauses are important tools for communication in our everyday lives. In this presentation, you did a great job of identifying an authentic subordinate clause and of commenting on its importance to the text message in which it was used. As you said, without the subordinate clause, your friends wouldn't have known why you were offering fries! Your reflection responses were also excellent: your statement about how this project showed you "that grammar is a part of real-world communication" and the corresponding examples you provide revealed your careful reflection on this topic. Wonderful job on this excellent work!

Figure 7.3 (Continued)

Instructional Recommendations

Let's now examine four instructional suggestions designed to help you assess your students' work on their grammar inquiries in meaningful and useful ways. The recommendations discussed here are:

1. Introduce the assessment criteria to students early in the grammar inquiry process.
2. Formatively assess students' understandings on the criteria throughout their grammar inquiry work,
3. Revisit the rubric criteria throughout the grammar inquiry process.
4. Use the assessment to recognize strengths and encourage future growth in specific ways.

In this section, we'll explore each of these recommendations individually.

Recommendation One: Introduce the Assessment Criteria to Students Early in the Grammar Inquiry Process

To facilitate students' successes on their grammar inquiries, I suggest sharing the assessment criteria with students early in their work on grammar inquiries so they can begin to understand what they'll be evaluated on at the conclusion of their inquiry projects. When you first introduce students to the grammar inquiry project using the information and ideas discussed in Chapter 1, you can also provide students with an initial look at these assessment criteria. When sharing these assessment criteria early on in the instructional process, I recommend making clear to students that they will revisit these criteria throughout their grammar inquiry work and that you'll continue to talk with them about ways to meet these criteria. This will ensure that students are aware of the criteria without overwhelming them. When you introduce these criteria to students, I also suggest making them available on an online learning platform the school uses, such as Google Classroom or a similar resource. By sharing the rubric this way, the students will be able to access it throughout the grammar inquiry process, which we'll discuss further in these instructional recommendations. Introducing students to these assessment criteria early in their grammar inquiries provides them with initial information about the goals they'll be striving to reach as they engage in their grammar inquiry work.

Recommendation Two: Formatively Assess Students' Understandings on the Criteria Throughout Their Grammar Inquiry Work

As students move through the many stages of the grammar inquiry process, I suggest formatively assessing them on their understandings of key rubric criteria. One especially significant "checkpoint" in the grammar inquiry process that lends itself well to formative assessments is described in Chapter 4, titled "Helping Students Identify and Analyze Authentic Examples of Grammatical Concepts." In this chapter, I discuss students completing a graphic organizer that asks them to identify the grammatical concept example they've found, state the context in which it was used, reflect on why the text's creator may have used the concept, and comment on how the text would be different if the concept was not used. I also recommend in that chapter to confer with students as they complete the graphic organizer to monitor their progress, note strengths of their existing work, and provide them with any needed support. These conferences provide an excellent opportunity with formative assessment on students' grammar inquiry work—they allow us teachers to monitor how well they're doing with important assessment criteria such as identifying authentic examples of their focal concept, analyzing their importance, and connecting their analyses to the essential question.

Another useful opportunity for formative assessment is found in the section of Chapter 6 that discusses opportunities for students to brainstorm their reflection ideas. While students brainstorm their insights on each of the reflection questions, we teachers can check in with them to provide feedback and support in the ideas and insights they've brainstormed. During these conversations, we can ask students to clarify ideas they've brainstormed, identify points they could further develop when they write their reflections, and praise particularly strong responses that they should include in the reflections they turn in. By talking with students about these reflection ideas, we can support their in-progress work and give them feedback that can help them maximize the effectiveness of their reflections. The students' brainstorms and our corresponding conversations with them about their ideas provide a valuable formative assessment opportunity that will help them craft strong reflections at the end of the inquiry process.

Recommendation Three: Revisit the Rubric Criteria Throughout the Grammar Inquiry Process

As students move through the grammar inquiry process, I recommend revisiting the rubric criteria regularly in order to remind students of these assessment standards and ensure that their work is developing in ways that correspond with the rubric components. I suggest reminding the students of the criteria at purposefully identified points throughout their work to help them be sure to keep these ideas in mind as their inquiries develop. For example, in addition to introducing students to the rubric criteria when you first talk with them about the grammar inquiry project, I suggest revisiting the rubric criteria at the following times during their inquiry work:

- Before they identify their own examples of authentically used grammatical concepts

- When they start to analyze the importance of the examples they identified
- When they begin to brainstorm their reflection ideas
- Before they give their inquiry presentations
- When they are finalizing their reflection statements.

When I revisit the rubric criteria with students, I discuss the rubric in general and then highlight any aspects that are particularly relevant to the work students are doing at the time. For example, when students are beginning to analyze the importance of the identified concepts, I give a brief overview of the rubric and then point out that the work they're doing at the time most relates to the rubric components that address the sections that relate to the student's analysis and their connection to the essential question. These discussions help students keep key evaluation criteria in mind while they work, which can enhance their ability to perform well on their inquiries.

Recommendation Four: Use the Assessment to Recognize Strengths and Encourage Future Growth in Specific Ways

My final recommendation for using the assessment rubric and criteria discussed in this chapter is to use this assessment tool to recognize specific strengths in students' grammar inquiry work and to be as specific as possible in identifying ways that students can continue to grow. This concrete information will convey to students the aspects of their grammar inquiries that are particularly strong, which will help them understand their literacy strengths that they can apply to future grammar inquiries and to other future English language arts work that they do. Concrete and specific feedback will also provide students with information about the ways they can improve their future literacy work. I suggest conveying these strengths and areas of future growth by using the "Strengths" and "Areas of Improvement" sections on the rubric depicted in Figure 7.1 as well as in the concluding comment that you share with the student. The examples of completed rubrics in Figures 7.2 and 7.3 show how I identified particular strengths and applicable areas of growth regarding my students' work. The concrete and specific feedback you give your students will allow for this assessment to be meaningful to them, which is a key goal of effective literacy assessment (NCTE, 2018), and will honor the work that each student did with useful, individualized feedback.

Key Takeaway Points

This section shares important points and insights to keep in mind as you assess your students' work on their grammar inquiries.

- At this stage in the grammar inquiry process, we provide our students with a summative evaluation of their grammar inquiry presentations and reflections.
- In order to assess students' work on their grammar inquiry projects, it's important to identify key evaluation components and tools that will help us evaluate their performance and give them meaningful feedback that communicates their areas of strength and of future growth.
- When I assess students' grammar inquiry presentations, I focus on the grammar inquiry presentation guidelines that I shared with students before they gave their presentations and use those guidelines to identify the key criteria on which I will assess the students' presentations.
- Similarly, when assessing students' reflections on their grammar inquiries, I use the grammar inquiry reflection guidelines that I previously shared with them to identify the criteria that I will use to evaluate their reflective work.
- Assessing students' work on their grammar inquiries in thoughtful and detailed ways is important for three key reasons:
  - It shows students that we value their work.
  - It communicates the strengths of their presentations and reflections.
  - It indicates how they can continue to develop.
- When assessing your students' work on their grammar inquiries, I recommend following these suggestions:
  - Introduce the assessment criteria to students early in the grammar inquiry process.
  - Formatively assess students' understandings on the criteria throughout their grammar inquiry work.
  - Revisit the rubric criteria throughout the grammar inquiry process.
  - Use the assessment to recognize strengths and encourage future growth in specific ways.
- The infographic in Figure 7.4 depicts these instructional recommendations.

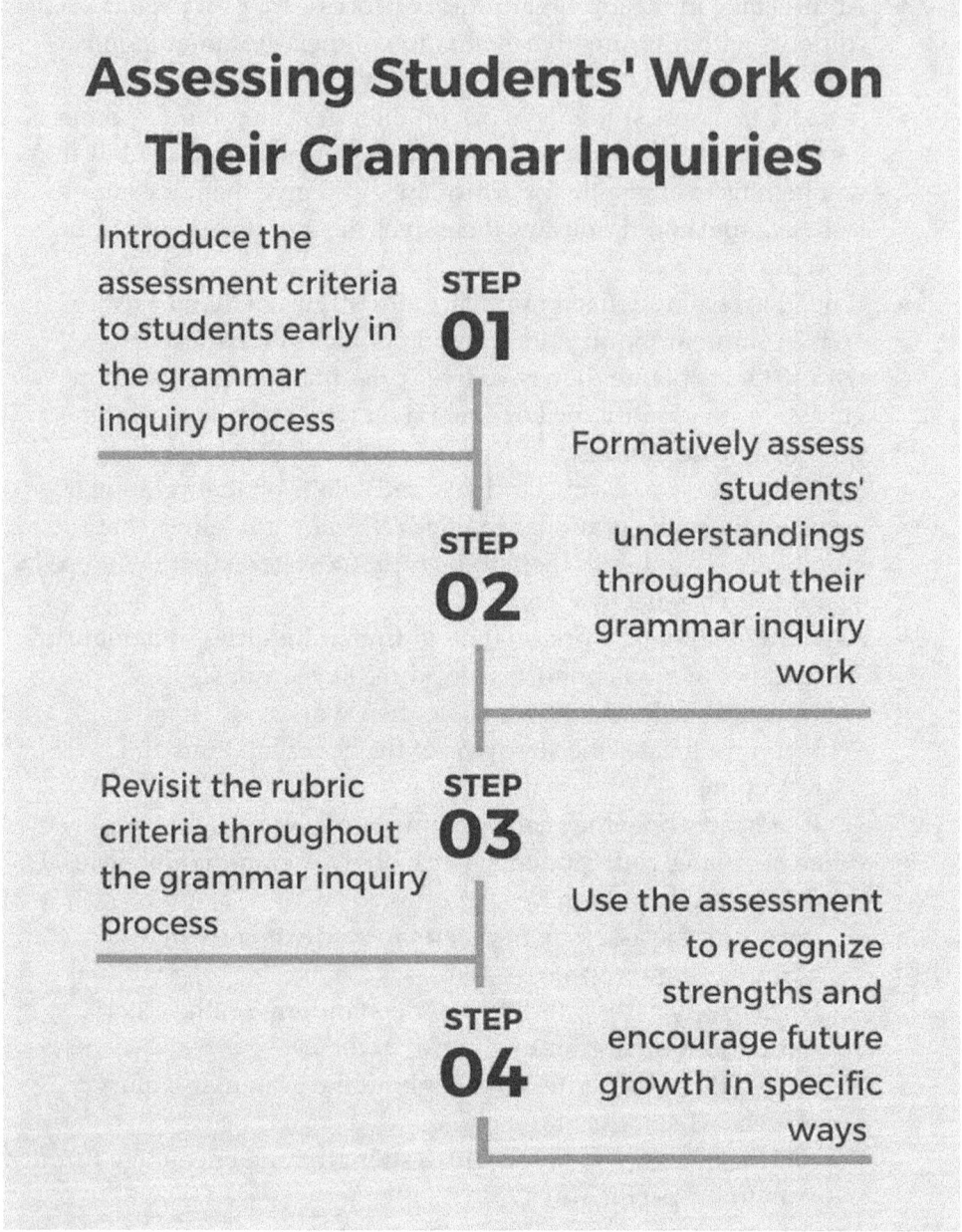

Figure 7.4 Infographic—Assessing Students' Work on Their Grammar Inquiries

8

Implementing This Approach
Suggestions for Classroom Practice

This chapter builds on the ideas, explanations, and recommendations presented in the previous ones. Now that we've examined all of the components of the grammar inquiry process, we'll now explore important suggestions designed to help you incorporate inquiry-based grammar instruction in your classroom. In this chapter, we'll look together at five essential suggestions for classroom practice. I'll discuss each one, provide a sample lesson plan that shows how key components of it can look in action, and share insights for putting it into practice. The suggestions for classroom practice discussed in this chapter are:

1. Discuss the fundamentals and importance of the focal concept.
2. Introduce students to their grammar inquiries.
3. Identify your own authentic example of a grammatical concept and have students help analyze its importance.
4. Support students as they identify and analyze authentic examples of grammatical concepts that align with the inquiry's essential question.
5. Construct opportunities for students to share their grammar inquiry findings and reflect on their experiences.

Let's now explore each of these suggestions in detail, examining its components, a relevant lesson and ideas for putting it into action.

Suggestion One: Discuss the Fundamentals and Importance of the Focal Concept

The first step I recommend taking is discussing with the students the fundamentals and the importance of the grammatical concept on which they'll focus in their inquiries. This provides students with foundational knowledge related to the focal concept and ensures that they all approach their inquiries with key common understandings of what the focal concept is and why it is used. As discussed in Chapter 1, when talking with students about the fundamentals of a concept, I conduct a mini-lesson that contains three key steps: 1) I introduce key features of the concept, 2) I provide engaging and accessible examples, and 3) I write the features and examples on anchor charts and post them in the classroom for reference throughout the inquiry and later in the school year. I emphasize to students that they don't need to memorize this information and that we'll be returning to it for further discussion throughout our work with the concept.

When talking with students about the importance of a grammatical concept, I like to show students published examples of the focal concept and discuss with them why that concept is significant to the published text in which it was used. For example, in Chapter 1 I discuss how, when talking with my tenth graders about the importance of subordinate clauses, I shared with them the following sentence from the book *The Hate U Give* by Angie Thomas (2017): "When my feet touch the cold floor, goose bumps pop all over me" (p. 31). After we read the sentence together, we discussed the subordinate clause "when my feet touch the cold floor," talking about the explanation and context that the clause provides. When doing this work with your students, I recommend identifying an example of the grammatical concept that they'll focus on in their inquiries from a published book that you feel they'll find accessible and interesting. After that, I suggest sharing that example with students and talking with them about the importance of the focal concept to the sentence, highlighting the kind of information it provides, why the author may have chosen to use it, and how the sentence would be different if the author did not use the grammatical concept.

Figure 8.1 contains an example lesson plan related to the identification and discussion of the importance of a grammatical concept to a published text. It is the plan that I used when talking with my tenth graders about the importance of the subordinate clause "When my feet touch the cold floor" in *The Hate U Give* by Angie Thomas.

> **Plan Topic:**
>
> - The importance of a published subordinate clause.
>
> **Key Learning Activities:**
>
> - Review anchor chart that discusses the features of subordinate clauses.
>
> - Display subordinate clause mentor text from *The Hate U Give* by Angie Thomas (2017): "When my feet touch the cold floor, goose bumps pop all over me" (p. 31).
>
> - Identify the subordinate clause "When my feet touch the cold floor."
>
> - Discussion: Why is the subordinate clause important to the sentence?
>
> - Follow up questions:
>
>   o What information does the subordinate clause provide?
>
>   o Why do you think Angie Thomas chose to use this subordinate clause in the sentence?
>
>   o Display revised version of the sentence with the subordinate clause removed. How is this sentence different from the original version? What do we not know? How is our experience as readers different?
>
> - Written reflection: Why do you think subordinate clauses can be important tools to effective communication?
>
> - Students share highlights from their reflections with partners. Volunteers share with the class.
>
> **Exit Question:**
>
> - What is something you noticed today about the importance of subordinate clauses to effective communication?

Figure 8.1 Example Lesson Plan One

Putting Suggestion One Into Practice

When putting this suggestion into action, I recommend keeping these instructional insights in mind:

- Use the introductory mini-lesson to share key information about the focal concept.
- Post key information from the mini-lesson for future reference.

- Share one or more published examples of the focal concept with students.
- Talk with students about the importance of the published example to the text in which it is used.
- Use this information to help students begin to explore the importance of the focal concept.

Suggestion Two: Introduce Students to Their Grammar Inquiries

My next recommendation for putting the ideas discussed in this book into action is to introduce students to the grammar inquiries that they'll be conducting. This builds off of the ideas they examined in the first suggestion, in which they looked at fundamental features of a grammatical concept and began to consider its significance by thinking about its importance to a published text. Now, in their inquiry-based work, students will begin to investigate essential questions about the importance of that concept to authentic language they encounter in their everyday lives. When introducing students to the work they'll do in their inquiries, I recommend first talking with them about the key features of the project. To do so, I share with students a description of the work they'll do in their grammar inquiries, such as the Subordinate Clause Grammar Inquiry Description found in Figure 1.1. When creating these descriptions for use with your students, I encourage you to include the following information:

- The grammar inquiry's essential question.
- Information on what students will do in their inquiries.
  - For example, in the Subordinate Clause Grammar Inquiry Description I shared with my students, I explained,

  > To conduct these inquiries, you'll look for examples of subordinate clauses in texts you encounter in your everyday lives, analyze the importance of those subordinate clauses to the texts in which they're used, and reflect on what you learned from the experience.

- Possible texts in which students might find the focal concept.

This is also an excellent time to give students a first look at the rubric on which you'll assess their grammar inquiry presentations and reflections so they have clear understandings of what they'll do in this project and the ways they'll be evaluated. Figure 8.2 contains an example lesson plan related to introducing

Plan Topic:

- Introduction to subordinate clause grammar inquiries.

Key Learning Activities:

- Reminders of previous work students have done with subordinate clauses.

- Review discussion: Students recall key ideas about what they've noticed so far from our discussions about the features and importance of subordinate clauses.

- Introduction grammar inquiry essential question: Why are subordinate clauses important tools for communication in our everyday lives?

- Introductory explanation of grammar inquiry: To conduct these inquiries, you'll look for examples of subordinate clauses in texts you encounter in your everyday lives, analyze the importance of those subordinate clauses to the texts in which they're used, and reflect on what you learned from the experience.

- Give students written Subordinate Clause Grammar Inquiry Description document and read it out loud.

- After reading the document with students, emphasize key inquiry components:

    o Students will identify subordinate clauses in texts they encounter in their everyday lives.

    o There are many possible texts in which subordinate clauses are used.

    o After students find an example of a subordinate clause in their everyday lives, they'll analyze its importance to the text in which they found it.

- Written reflection: Students reflect on what they notice about the grammar inquiry description.

- Discussion: Key ideas that stand out to students, what interests them about the work, and what questions they have.

- Share with students introductory information about the presentation students will give, the reflection they will write, and key assessment criteria.

Exit Questions:

- What is something about today's discussion of the grammar inquiry project that most interests you? What is a question you have about it?

Figure 8.2 Example Lesson Plan Two

grammar inquiries to students. It is the plan I used when introducing my tenth-graders to their subordinate clause grammar inquiries. When conducting similar lessons with your students about different concepts, I recommend keeping the core components of the lesson while substituting the focal concept on which the students will focus.

Putting Suggestion Two Into Practice

When putting the ideas in this suggestion into action in your instruction, I recommend keeping the following ideas in mind:

- Review with students the previous work they've done with the focal concept, highlighting key points with them about its features and importance.
- Introduce the essential question of the grammar inquiry that students will conduct.
- Provide an introductory overview explanation of the grammar inquiry.
- Share a written description of the grammar inquiry with students, highlighting key aspects that you most want to introduce them to.
- Provide introductory information about the final products students will create at the conclusion of the inquiry.

Suggestion Three: Identify Your Own Authentic Example of a Grammatical Concept and Have Students Help Analyze its Importance

Now that you've introduced your students to their grammar inquiries, I recommend demonstrating for them what key aspects of this work look like. To do so, I suggest identifying a real-world example of the grammatical concept that the students will be focusing on in their inquiries, sharing it and discussing it with students, and then talking with students about the importance of that grammatical concept to the text in which it was used. This gives students experience and background in thinking about authentically used grammatical concepts and shows them what they will be doing in their own grammar inquiries. By sharing with students examples of real-world grammatical concepts that you've identified from your own language experiences and talking with them about the importance of those concepts, you'll help them understand the steps they'll take and the thinking they'll do as they engage in the grammar inquiry process.

For example, as discussed in Chapter 2, before my seventh-graders conducted grammar inquiries focused on strong verbs, I provided them with two examples of strong verb use from a conversation I had with one of my children about a football game. I shared two sentences, one containing the strong verb "sprinted" and the other featuring the word "rushed." I first displayed a sentence from the conversation that included "sprinted," which read "Najee Harris sprinted past the defense!," and thought aloud about why this word meets the criteria of a strong verb. After that, I shared the sentence containing the strong verb "rushed" ("The players rushed onto the field to join the celebration") and asked students to identify the strong verb in the sentence and explain why it meets the criteria for this grammatical concept. Afterwards, as discussed in Chapter 3, I engaged the students in a discussion of the importance of these strong verbs to the sentences in which they were used. I led these discussions by asking my students to reflect on and talk about two related topics: why we think my son may have used these strong verbs in our conversation about the football game, and how each statement would be different if he didn't use the strong verbs that he did. These discussion topics helped the students think carefully about the importance of each of these authentically used strong verbs. Similarly, when working with my tenth-graders, I identified subordinate clauses that I used in a conversation with a friend about running a road race. I shared these examples with my students, worked with them on identifying why they represent subordinate clauses, and facilitated conversations about their importance to our discussion of running the race.

Figure 8.3 depicts a sample lesson plan for discussing with students the importance of real-world examples of grammatical concepts. It is the same plan I used when talking with my seventh-graders about the significance of the strong verbs I shared with them. When doing this work with your students, I recommend using this plan as a model to help you structure these types of discussions about the importance of the grammatical concepts you share with them.

Putting Suggestion Three Into Practice

I recommend keeping the following ideas in mind when putting this suggestion into action in the classroom:

- Identify an example from your own authentic communication of the grammatical concept students are focusing on in their grammar inquiries.
- Share the example with students and talk with them about why it is an example of the focal concept.
- Discuss with students why the concept is important to the effectiveness of the text in which it was used.
- Help students reflect on how the original text would be different without the use of the focal concept.

Plan Topic:

- The significance of authentically used strong verbs.

Key Learning Activities:

- As students enter, display the focal question, "Strong verbs in the real world: Why are they important?"

- Review of work from previous class: Remind students that, in the previous class, they looked at two examples of strong verbs used in real-world situations.

- Introduce the day's focus: Today, we're going to think further about those strong verb examples: since we identified them in our last conversation, we're going to talk today about why they are so important.

- Display first strong verb example, "Najee Harris sprinted past the defense!," calling attention to the strong verb "sprinted."

- Share initial discussion question related to this example, "Why did my son use the strong verb 'sprinted' in this conversation?," and ask students to take two minutes and write a response to the question. Provide students with an additional prompt to encourage their thinking: "When writing on this topic, you might think about why he felt using this strong verb might make the sentence better and more effective."

- Students share responses with partners; volunteers share with the class. As students share their responses, call attention to particularly strong insights and ask follow-up questions when relevant.

- Share next discussion question related to this example: "How would the statement be different if my son didn't use that strong verb?"
    - After sharing this question with students, display the original version of the sentence, "Najee Harris sprinted past the defense!," and a revised version that does not contain the strong verb: "Najee Harris went past the defense!"

- Ask students to take two minutes and write how they think the use of the strong verb "sprinted" impacted the sentence and how the two versions are different.

- Students share responses with partners, and volunteers share with the class. Praise particularly strong responses and follow up on students' statements as relevant.

- Display second strong verb example, "The players rushed on the field to join the celebration," calling attention to the strong verb "rushed."

Figure 8.3 Example Lesson Plan Three

(Continued)

- Share initial discussion question related to this example, "Why do you think my son used the strong verb 'rushed' in this statement?" and ask students to take two minutes to write a response to the question. Encourage students to consider what impact this strong verb might have had on the effectiveness of the sentence.

- Students share responses with partners; volunteers share their ideas with the class. Identify strong statements and ask follow up questions.

- Share second discussion question related to this example: "How would this statement be different if my son didn't use this strong verb?
   - After sharing this question, display the original text, "The players rushed onto the field to join the celebration," as well as a revised version without the strong verb that reads "The players moved onto the field to join the celebration."

- Ask students to take two minutes and write how they think the strong verb "rushed" impacted the sentence and how the two versions are different.

- Students share responses with partners, and volunteers share with the class. Call attention to especially insightful responses and engage students in follow-up discussion when applicable.

Exit Question:

- What did our work today show you about the importance of strong verbs to real-world communication?

Figure 8.3 (Continued)

Suggestion Four: Support Students As They Identify and Analyze Authentic Examples of Grammatical Concepts That Align with the Inquiry's Essential Question

This suggestion is designed to help you guide your students as they take increased ownership of their grammar inquiry work. At this point in the grammar inquiry process, students move from the identification and analysis-related discussions they have had up to this point to truly embarking on their own inquiries. As discussed in Chapter 4 of this book, there are three related activities for students to do that will help them conduct these inquiries: 1) Review the essential question they'll explore in their inquiry, 2) Identify authentically used examples of the concept on which they're focusing, and 3) Analyze the importance of the grammatical concept they identified to the context in which it was used. These three steps will create opportunities for students to identify and analyze real-world examples of their focal concepts.

As teachers, we can support our students through this work by helping them with each of these steps. First, we can work with our students as they review the essential questions that guide their inquiries, talking with them about what the question means, how their investigation of it can look in action, and why the question is important to their understanding of the focal concept and to their experiences with language. After that, we can support our students as they identify authentically used examples of the focal concept. As I described in Chapter 4, I recommend first exploring with them a variety of examples of everyday situations in which they might find the focal concept, asking for their input during this discussion, and then writing the ideas on a piece of chart paper to post in the classroom. Once you have discussed these possibilities with students, I suggest asking them to explore the texts and situations of their choice with the goal of finding real-world examples of the focal concept. I create space in class for students to reflect and try to identify examples of the concept in their everyday lives, but I also ask them to take time outside of school to make these identifications since grammatical concepts are so important to texts they engage with outside of school.

Next, once students have identified authentic examples of the grammatical concept they're focusing on in their inquiries, the next step is for them to analyze the importance of that concept. During these analyses, students think carefully about the importance of the concept they've identified to the context in which it was used. To help students reflect on the importance of the grammatical concept they've identified, I ask them to think about two questions: 1) Why the creator of the text may have used the concept, and 2) How the text would be different if the concept was not used. Figure 4.1 (available in Chapter 4 and in Appendix B) contains a graphic organizer that students can use to organize their identifications and analyses of authentically used grammatical concepts. It asks students to identify the grammatical concept example they found, state the context in which it was used, discuss why the text's creator may have used the concept, and comment on how the text would be different if the concept was not used.

Figure 8.4 contains a sample lesson plan that focuses on students analyzing the importance of the grammatical concept they identified. It is the same plan I used when working with my seventh-graders as they analyzed the significance of the strong verbs they found. The plan focuses a great deal on students working on their analyses while I confer with them to support their work.

Plan Topic:

- Students' analyses of authentically used strong verbs they identified.

Key Learning Activities:

- Review discussion from previous class, noting that the class reviewed the essential question, brainstormed situations in which we can find strong verbs in our out-of-school lives, and began to think about examples of strong verbs in authentic, real-world situations.

- Introduce the day's focus, telling students that we're going to build off our previous experiences by talking about their identifications and analyses of strong verbs they found.

- Introduce the graphic organizer depicted in Figure 4.1, telling students that the graphic organizer asks them to list the strong verb they found, write the context in which it was used, share their thoughts on why the text's creator may have used that strong verb, and then write how they think the text would be different if that strong verb wasn't used.

- Project the graphic organizer to the screen at the front of the room and give each student a paper copy of it.

- Tell students that as they work on recording their identifications analyses on the graphic organizer, I will check in with them to see how they're doing, answer any questions they have, and provide other support.

- Circulate the classroom, checking with students as they work. During these conferences, call attention to strengths of students' identifications and analyses and point out any areas for growth or further development. If students are struggling analyzing why the text's creator may have used the concept or how the text would be different without the focal concept, ask them probing questions to facilitate their ideas and reflections on this work.

- Confer with as many students as possible, keeping record of the students you talked to, brief summaries of their identifications and analyses, strengths of their work, and areas for future growth.

- Once you've finished conferring with students, ask them to talk with partners about their identifications and analyses.

- Praise students' work on their identifications and analyses before asking them to respond to the exit question.

Exit Question:

- What is a reason why the strong verb example you identified is important to the text in which it was used?

Figure 8.4 Example Lesson Plan Four

Putting Suggestion Four Into Practice
When putting the information in this suggestion into practice in your classroom, I recommend keeping these ideas in mind:

- Work with students as they review the essential questions that guide their inquiries.
- Support students as they identify authentically used examples of the focal concept they're studying in their inquiries.
- Create opportunities for students to analyze the importance of the focal grammatical concept.
- Confer with students as they analyze the significance of the concepts they identified, praising strengths of their work and providing any relevant support.

Suggestion Five: Construct Opportunities for Students to Share Their Grammar Inquiry Findings and Reflect on Their Experiences

This final suggestion focuses on the ways students will share key findings and reflections from their grammar inquiry work. Specifically, I recommend creating ways for students to present the results of their grammar inquiries and then reflect on their experiences with this work. As discussed in Chapter 5, when constructing opportunities for students to share their grammar inquiry findings, I like to organize community-oriented events for students to share their grammar inquiry results through presentations that describe what they learned in their inquiries. When planning for these events, I invite other English classes in the school and students' caregivers to attend, and I make a flyer for students to share with and invite others that they would like to attend. To help students succeed in these presentations, I recommend providing them with clear expectations for their presentations, such as the suggested length of the presentation, multimedia guidelines, and information about how the presentation should incorporate key inquiry components such as the essential question, the example the students identified, and their analysis of it. I also remind students of key components of the grammar inquiry rubric that relate to their presentation work.

After students have given these presentations, I recommend creating opportunities for students to reflect on what they've learned in their grammar inquiries and why that knowledge is important. As discussed in Chapter 6, when students reflect on their grammar inquiry experiences, I ask them to craft written responses to two related reflection questions: 1) What did you learn about the focal concept by identifying and analyzing real-world examples of it? and 2) Why is what you learned in the grammar inquiry project important? To help students create these reflections, I suggest organizing ways for them to brainstorm their thoughts on each of these reflection questions. When

I constructed these brainstorming experiences for my students, I introduced each question to them, asked them to write down some initial thoughts related to those questions, and provided them with graphic organizers they could use as they generate these ideas. (The graphic organizer I gave students related to the first reflection question is depicted in Figure 6.3, and the organizer associated with the second question is in Figure 6.4. Both are also available in Appendix B.) I told my students that these graphic organizers are possible ways to express the ideas they have, but they can also brainstorm in other ways, such as making lists, freewriting, or using another way to record their thinking. After students brainstorm their ideas about the reflection questions, I talk with them about key guidelines for their reflection responses. In these guidelines, I share information about a suggested length for their responses and emphasize that the reflections should contain students' own insights along with support from specific examples from their inquiry work. This is also a good time to remind students of the rubric criteria that relate to their reflective work.

Figure 8.5 depicts an example lesson plan related to students' brainstorming ideas connected to their grammar inquiry reflections. It is the plan I used when helping my seventh-graders brainstorm their thoughts on reflection questions related to their strong verb inquiries.

Plan Topic:

- Students brainstorm ideas related to grammar inquiry reflection questions.

Key Learning Activities:

- Review previous class's discussion, in which I introduced students to the idea of reflecting on their grammar inquiries. In this discussion, I told students that they would be answering reflection questions on their grammar inquiries and talked with them about why reflection is important to learning. Remind of highlights from this conversation to contextualize the work they'll do in today's class.

- Introduce first reflection question to students: "What did you learn about the focal concept of strong verbs by identifying and analyzing real world examples of it?"

- Ask students to brainstorm some ideas about what they learned about strong verbs in their grammar inquiries and how they know they learned that information.

- Display "Reflection Question One Brainstorm Template" (available in Figure 6.3 and in Appendix B) on the projector screen and give each student a copy. Discuss the key features of the brainstorm template with students.

- Explain to students that this is one option for brainstorming their ideas, but they can also brainstorm in other ways, such as making lists, freewriting, or using another way to record their thinking. Tell students they can also use the graphic organizer in different ways, such as not completing every circle or even adding extra if they have other ideas they want to express.

Figure 8.5 Example Lesson Plan Five

(Continued)

- While students brainstorm their ideas, check in with them to provide support, asking questions when relevant and praising strong responses.

- Introduce second reflection to students: "Why is what you learned in the grammar inquiry project important?"

- Talk with students about how this question is different from the first one they responded to, calling attention to the way that the first reflection question asks them what they learned while this one asks them to reflect on what that they learned was important.

- Ask students to brainstorm possible ideas and responses related to this question by noting their thoughts about why what they learned in the grammar inquiry project is important and why they think so.
- Display "Reflection Question Two Brainstorm Template" (available in Figure 6.4 and in Appendix B) on the projector screen and give each student a copy. Discuss the key features of the brainstorm template with students.

- Explain to students that this is one option for brainstorming their ideas, but they can also brainstorm in other ways, such as making lists, freewriting, or using another way to record their thinking. Tell students they can also use the graphic organizer in different ways, such as not completing every circle or even adding extra if they have other ideas they want to express.

- While students brainstorm their ideas, check in with them to provide support, asking questions when relevant and praising strong responses.

Exit Question:

- What is an idea you brainstormed today that especially stands out to you?

Figure 8.5 (Continued)

Putting Suggestion Five Into Practice

When putting the ideas discussed in suggestion five into action in your classroom, I recommend keeping the following insights in mind:

- ◆ Create opportunities for students to present the results of their grammar inquiries with audiences that go beyond the class, such as other English classes, students' caregivers, and other community members the students choose to invite.
- ◆ To help students succeed in these presentations, I recommend providing them with clear expectations for their presentations and reviewing relevant aspects of the assessment rubric you'll use to evaluate their work.
- ◆ After students have given these presentations, I recommend creating opportunities for students to reflect on what they've learned in their grammar inquiries and why that knowledge is important.

- To help students reflect on these ideas, share the reflection questions with them and build in time for them to brainstorm their responses to these questions.
- After students brainstorm their reflection ideas, talk with them about guidelines and expectations for the reflection responses they'll create, highlighting relevant information from the assessment rubric.

Final Thoughts on Implementing This Approach

The ideas shared in this chapter will provide you with key recommendations and insights for putting the grammar inquiry approach into action in your teaching. By incorporating the five key suggestions discussed here, you will equip your students with important knowledge of the concept they'll focus on in their grammar inquiries, help them understand the work they'll do in their inquiries, model key aspects of the inquiry process, and support them as they engage in their own inquiry work. The explanations, sample plans, and instructional recommendations featured in this chapter are designed to be a user-friendly resource for you as you put the grammar inquiry approach described in this book into action. This information, which synthesizes key ideas shared throughout the book, can be a useful point of reference as you engage your students in inquiry- and asset-based grammar instruction.

Conclusion

Why Inquiry- and Asset-Based Grammar Instruction Makes a Difference

Throughout this book, we've explored key features of inquiry- and asset-based grammar instruction, examining ideas such as what it is, how it can look in practice, and essential recommendations to consider when incorporating it into your own instruction. This concluding chapter provides closing insights that convey the importance of this approach to providing students with student-centered and meaningful grammar instruction that draws on the assets and experiences they bring to the classroom. The chapter highlights four reasons why inquiry- and asset-based grammar instruction is particularly important and should be incorporated in today's schools.

1. It centers students.
2. It moves grammar instruction from deficit-based to asset-based.
3. It incorporates the power of essential questions.
4. It prepares students for authentic engagement with language.

In this chapter, we'll examine each of these reasons, discussing how it applies to grammar inquiry work and how each one conveys the impact that inquiry- and asset-based grammar instruction can have on our students.

It Centers Students

An especially significant aspect of the grammar inquiry process is that it centers students. Instead of placing a grammar textbook or out-of-context worksheets at the center of their experiences with grammar instruction, this approach emphasizes students' real-world experiences with the grammatical concept on which they're focusing. When we utilize inquiry- and asset-based approaches to grammar instruction in our classrooms, we send a message to students that we value their real-world experiences with language and the texts, media, and forms of communication that are central to those experiences. These opportunities for students to engage with the language they encounter in their everyday lives put them and their lived experiences at the center of their grammar instruction. It makes their work with grammar culturally relevant by using students' cultures and authentic experiences to support their learning (Ladson-Billings, 1995). In addition, it creates a culturally sustaining (Paris, 2012) environment by valuing and incorporating the many cultures and identities that can be represented in students' authentic language uses. Grammar inquiries incorporate these principles by emphasizing that grammatical concepts are part of our everyday lives and are central to our authentic experiences with language. They are essential aspects of all of the texts with which our students engage. By working with grammar in this way, students can see their interests and experiences reflected in grammar instruction in ways they have not before.

It Moves Grammar Instruction from Deficit-Based to Asset-Based

Another important aspect of inquiry- and asset-based grammar work is the way that it shifts grammar instruction away from deficit-oriented approaches and toward experiences that incorporate students' assets. Deficit approaches to grammar instruction focus primarily on factual recall and out-of-context activities. This out-of-context approach, which emphasizes worksheets and rote memorization, has traditionally characterized grammar instruction (Weaver, 1998). Conversely, asset-based instruction approaches teaching and learning in ways that focus on real-world connections to classroom material and authentic applications of students' knowledge (New York University, 2020). The asset-based approach to grammar instruction described in this book is designed to provide students with meaningful opportunities to engage with grammatical concepts. Asset-based teaching and learning provides students with more equitable opportunities to succeed than traditional deficit-based approaches by providing opportunities for authentic connections and applications of what they learn (New York University, 2020).

Grammar inquiries are an outstanding way to disrupt deficit-based approaches to the teaching and learning of grammar and move toward an asset-based experience. This approach applies the principles of asset-based teaching and learning to grammar instruction by helping students see grammar as an opportunity to apply their knowledge of grammatical concepts to authentic communication in their communities and out-of-school contexts. When we position the teaching and learning of grammar as relevant to all of our students' real-world encounters with language, we communicate to students that their lived experiences have an important role in the classroom. Viewing students' cultures and backgrounds as assets to their learning is an important way to create inclusive and supportive learning environments that help them succeed (Milner, 2011). When our students engage in grammar inquiries, we shift the focus of their grammar instruction away from out-of-context activities and rote memorization and toward meaningful applications of their understandings of what grammatical concepts are and why they are important to their authentic experiences with language.

It Incorporates the Power of Essential Questions

Inquiry- and asset-based grammar instruction is also meaningful because of its use of essential questions. These thought-provoking, big-picture questions call for higher-order thinking and point students toward important ideas that are transferable to other contexts and situations (McTighe & Wiggins, 2013). While inquiry-based learning that uses essential questions to encourage students to think deeply about academic topics has been used in a variety of subject areas, the connection to grammar instruction described in this book is a new application of it. Grammar inquiries capitalize on the power of essential questions by connecting them to the impact and significance of grammatical concepts to authentic, real-world communication. For example, the seventh-grade English class discussed in this book investigated the essential question "How do strong verbs make the texts we encounter outside of school as effective as possible?" and the tenth graders considered the question "Why are subordinate clauses important tools for communication in our everyday lives?"

Both of these questions facilitated the thought-provoking experiences and the engagement with higher-order thinking that McTighe and Wiggins (2013) describe. They established a meaningful learning framework that guided students' identifications and analyses of real-world examples of the grammatical concepts they studied. Students returned to these questions throughout the inquiries, considering them from the beginning of their inquiry experiences all the way through their culminating presentations and reflections. Without these essential questions, students would not be able to engage with the focal concepts in in-depth and meaningful ways. The essential questions function as entry points into the deep and meaningful work that students do throughout their inquiries. In addition, they work as guideposts that give students the guidance and structure that they need to successfully complete their inquiries. Essential questions maximize the learning benefits of grammar inquiries and help students think in nuanced and complex ways about their focal concepts.

It Prepares Students for Authentic Engagement with Language

Finally, inquiry- and asset-based grammar instruction is beneficial because it prepares students to engage authentically with language in the future. A key principle of grammar inquiry work is that grammar does not just exist in textbooks, on worksheets, and in other school-created activities: it is living in the world around us, making our real-world communication as effective and impactful as possible. By engaging with authentic uses of language and exploring the importance of grammatical concepts to real-world communication, students develop a deep understanding of grammar and language that goes well beyond one assignment. When my students studied the importance of strong verbs and subordinate clauses to effective communication in their everyday lives, they learned about more than just those concepts: they also learned how grammatical concepts on the whole are essential to authentic communication. The students developed the ability to identify real-world examples of grammatical concepts, analyze why the creators of those texts used them, and consider how the texts would be different without the usage of those concepts. These are skills and tools that they can apply to all of their experiences with language that will serve them well throughout their lives.

Final Thoughts

Inquiry- and asset-based grammar instruction can reshape students' experiences with grammar, providing them meaningful learning opportunities that center them, incorporate their assets, and help them think deeply about the importance of grammar to authentic communication. In this book, I've shared key ideas, instructional steps, and resources to use when incorporating this approach into action in your middle- or high-school English classroom. The information described here will help you engage your students with grammar in thought-provoking, culturally relevant (Ladson-Billings,

1995), and culturally sustaining (Paris, 2012) ways. Since meaningful grammar instruction is especially challenging (Ruday, 2020c; Weaver, 1998), the ideas, information, and resources available to you in this book will help you make a significant impact on your students' experiences with grammar. I am thrilled that you have used this resource to learn about inquiry-based grammar instruction. I would love to hear about your experiences and provide any support I can!

References

Chang, B. (2019). Reflection in learning. *Online Learning, 23*(1), 95–110.

Cushman, K. (2003). *Fires in the bathroom: Advice for teachers from high school students.* The New Press.

Flavell, J. H. (1979). Metacognition and cognitive monitoring. *American Psychologist, 34,* 906–911.

Fletcher, R., & Portalupi, J. (2001). *Writing workshop: The essential guide.* Heinemann.

Fluckiger, J. (2010). Single point rubric: A tool for responsible student self-assessment. *Teacher Education Faculty Publications, 5.*

Garner, R. (1987). *Metacognition and reading comprehension.* Ablex.

Helyer, R. (2015). Learning through reflection: The critical role of reflection in work-based learning (WBL). *Journal of Work-Applied Management, 7*(1), 15–27.

Ladson-Billings, G. (1995). But that's just good teaching! The case for culturally relevant pedagogy. *Theory into Practice, 34*(3), 159–165.

Lee, V. S. (2012). What is inquiry-guided learning? *New Directions for Teaching and Learning, 129,* 5–14.

McTighe, J., & Wiggins, G. (2013). *Essential questions: Opening doors to student understanding.* ASCD.

Milner, R. (2011). Culturally relevant pedagogy in a diverse urban classroom. *The Urban Review, 43*(1), 66–89.

National Council of Teachers of English. (2018). *Literacy assessment: Definitions, principles, and practices* (Position Statement.) Retrieved from https://ncte.org/statement/assessmentframingst/

New York University Steinhardt School of Education. (2020, September 16). An asset-based approach to education: What it is and why it matters. Teacher Education Reinvented. https://teachereducation.steinhardt.nyu.edu/an-asset-based-approach-to-education-what-it-is-and-why-it-matters/

Paris, D. (2012). Culturally sustaining pedagogy: A needed change in stance, terminology, and practice. *Educational Researcher, 41*(3), 93–97.

Ruday, S. (2020a). Grammar, ownership, and usefulness: Student-centered inquiries into authentic uses of grammatical concepts through the grammar inquiry project. *Virginia English Journal, 69*(2), 22–28.

Ruday, S. (2020b). Grammar without walls: Student-centered and culturally relevant grammar instruction for the present and future of literacy. *Literacy Today*, *38*(2), 51–52.

Ruday, S. (2020c). *The middle school grammar toolkit: Using mentor texts to teach standards-based language and grammar in grades 6–8*. Routledge Eye on Education.

Ruday, S., & Caprino, K. (2020). *Inquiry-based literature instruction in the 6–12 Classroom: A hands-on guide for deeper learning*. Routledge Eye on Education.

Ruday, S., & Caprino, K. (2022). *Student-centered literacy assessment in the 6–12 classroom: An asset-based approach*. Routledge Eye on Education.

Saeed, A. (2022). *Omar rising*. Nancy Paulsen Books.

Thomas, A. (2017). *The hate U give*. Balzer + Bray.

Weaver, C. (1998). Teaching grammar in the context of writing. In C. Weaver (Ed.), *Lessons to Share on Teaching Grammar in Context* (pp. 18–38). Heinemann.

Wiggins, G., & McTighe, J. (2005). *Understanding by design*. Pearson.

Appendix A
A Guide for Book Studies

This resource provides discussion questions to prompt conversation for teachers engaging in a professional book study with this text. It contains questions to reflect on after reading each of the book's chapters. If you read this book with colleagues, I encourage you to talk together about these questions and your responses to them as you consider the ideas presented in this book. If you are reading the book on your own, I suggest reflecting on these questions to help you think in depth about the ideas presented in the text. Whether you are reading the book collaboratively or independently, these questions will help you engage with and reflect on key concepts and information in the book. Depending on your preference, you can consider the questions chapter-by-chapter as you read the book, or you can wait until you've completed the book to reflect on the questions. I hope these questions provide you with enriching and useful reflection on the inquiry- and asset-based approach to grammar instruction described in this book!

Introduction: Using Students' Inquiries and Assets in Grammar Instruction

1. What stands out to you about the description in the beginning of this book of a seventh-grade English class sharing the results of their grammar inquiries?
2. What challenges have you faced when teaching grammar?
3. What are some key benefits that you believe inquiry-based learning could have for your students?
4. Why can it be important to incorporate our students' assets, cultures, and experiences in the English classroom?
5. How can students' assets and experiences be especially important to teaching grammar?

Chapter 1: Building the Foundation for Inquiry-Based and Asset-Focused Grammar Instruction

1. This chapter discusses the significance of building students' fundamental knowledge of grammatical concepts. What is a grammatical concept that you might teach to your students? What are some of its key features? Give examples.
2. The chapter also recommends showing students some published examples of the focal concept and talking with them about the importance of those published examples. What is a published example of a grammatical concept that you might teach to your students? Why do you think the grammatical concept in this example is important?
3. What stands out to you about the Subordinate Clause Grammar Inquiry Description in Figure 1.1?
4. What are some key points you will emphasize for your students when introducing grammar inquiries to them?
5. In the "Instructional Recommendations" in this chapter, I recommend that teachers "Explain to students that grammar inquiries are authentic applications of their grammatical insights." Why can it be important for students to have authentic applications of grammar?

Chapter 2: Showing Students Examples of Authentically Used Grammatical Concepts

1. Figure 2.1 lists some texts where we can find grammatical concepts in our out-of-school lives. What are some texts that you think could contain examples of a grammatical concept you might teach to your students?
2. What is an example from your everyday communication of a grammatical concept that you have taught your students or might teach them in the future?
3. This chapter explains that showing students examples of authentically used grammatical concepts is important in part because doing so provides a model for students' own identifications of grammatical concepts in their grammar inquiries. How could modeling this work help students?
4. Take a look at the examples of grammatical concepts that I shared with students in the "How Can It Look in Action?" section. What stands out to you about these examples?

5. One of the instructional recommendations in this chapter is to "Help students understand the features of the examples you share." How might you help your students understand the features of a real-world example of a grammatical concept that you share with them?

Chapter 3: Reflecting with Students on the Importance of Authentically Used Grammatical Concepts

1. A key aspect of reflecting with students on the importance of authentically used grammatical concepts is to discuss with students why the creator of the text may have used this concept. Why could this be an important topic to discuss with students?
2. Another key aspect of this reflective work is to talk with students about how the text would be different if the concept was not used. Why do you think discussing this idea could be important?
3. Think about the example from your everyday communication of a grammatical concept that you have taught your students or might teach them in the future. Why do you think this example is important to the text in which it was used? How do you think the text would be different without it?
4. One of the instructional recommendations shared in this chapter is to "Create space for students to consider the importance of the concepts" that you share with them. Why do you think it is important to create this space?
5. Another instructional suggestion presented in this chapter is to "Discuss with students that they will apply this same analytical approach to their own inquiries." Based on the information in this chapter and your own ideas, what are some points you will emphasize when discussing this information with your students?

Chapter 4: Helping Students Identify and Analyze Authentic Examples of Grammatical Concepts

1. One of the first activities described in this chapter is to review with students the essential question they'll explore in their inquiries. What is an essential question you might ask your students to consider in a grammar inquiry?
2. What are some texts you think your students might examine when looking for authentic examples of a grammatical concept?

3. This chapter points out that grammar instruction has traditionally focused on memorization of terms and out-of-context worksheets (Weaver, 1998). What are some benefits of making grammar instruction relevant to students' real-world communication?
4. The "How Can It Look in Action?" section in this chapter describes my experiences conferring with students as they analyze the importance of the authentically used grammatical concept they identified. What are some strategies you will use to confer with your students about grammatical concept examples they identify and analyze?
5. When my students began conducting grammar inquiries, I became very excited about the work they would do! What is something about teaching students in this way that most excites you?

Chapter 5: Creating Opportunities for Students to Share Their Findings

1. One key idea discussed in this chapter is organizing community events where students will share the results of their inquiries. What are some ways that you will spread the word about students' inquiry presentations?
2. What are some challenges you foresee with organizing events where students will present their inquiries? How will you address these challenges?
3. Another important part of students presenting their inquiries is providing them with clear guidelines for the inquiry presentations. What are some guidelines you will share with students before they present their inquiries?
4. This chapter discusses how students' inquiry presentations can be meaningful and motivational for them. How do you think your students might find meaning and motivation in sharing their grammar inquiries with a broad audience as discussed in this chapter?
5. Examine the instructional examples of grammar inquiry presentations in the "How Can It Look in Action?" section. What is something that stands out to you from the descriptions of these events and of the student work featured in these sections?

Chapter 6: Asking Students to Reflect on Their Experiences

1. How have you used reflection in your teaching before? What are some challenges and successes you experienced when helping your students reflect?
2. The first reflection question described in this chapter is "What did you learn about the focal concept by identifying and analyzing real-world examples of it?" What do you think students can learn from reflecting on this question?
3. The second reflection question discussed in this chapter is "Why is what you learned in the grammar inquiry project important?" What do you think are some benefits that can come from answering this reflection question?
4. What do you notice about the student reflection examples shared in this chapter? How could they be useful to you as you encourage your students to conduct their own reflections?
5. One of the chapter's instructional recommendations is to model your own reflections. What are some ideas you might emphasize when you model reflecting for your students?

Chapter 7: Assessing Students' Work on Their Grammar Inquiries

1. This chapter reviews the guidelines I shared with students before they presented their grammar inquiry results. What are some guidelines that you would give your students before they present their grammar inquiries?
2. The chapter also includes the guidelines I shared with students before they wrote their grammar inquiry reflections. What are some reflection guidelines that you feel would be especially important to share with your students?
3. What are some aspects of the grammar inquiry rubric depicted in Figure 7.1 that especially stand out to you?
4. In this chapter, I describe three key reasons why the grammar inquiry assessment practice discussed here is important: it shows students that we value their work; it communicates the strengths of their presentations and reflections; and it indicates how they can continue to develop. Select one of these statements and comment on why you think it is especially meaningful for an effective assessment.

5. In the "Instructional Recommendations" section in this chapter, I suggest formatively assessing students' understandings on the rubric criteria throughout their grammar inquiry work. What are some ways you might formatively assess students' understandings throughout their grammar inquiries?

Chapter 8: Implementing This Approach: Suggestions for Classroom Practice

1. Based on the description, sample lesson plan, and instructional recommendations described in this chapter, what are some key practices you will use when discussing with your students the fundamentals and importance of a focal concept?
2. Drawing on the information in this chapter, what are some strategies you will use when introducing your students to their grammar inquiries? What will you most emphasize and explain to them?
3. Using the suggestions and other details in this chapter as a guide, what are some tactics you will use when helping your students understand and analyze the authentic example of the focal concept that you share with them?
4. What are some ideas and instructional practices that you will incorporate in your teaching when you help your students identify and analyze authentic examples of grammatical concepts?
5. What are some steps you will take to support your students as they share their grammar inquiry findings and reflect on their experiences?

Conclusion: Why Inquiry- and Asset-Based Grammar Instruction Makes a Difference

1. This chapter discusses how inquiry- and asset-based grammar instruction centers students. What are some reasons why you feel it can be important to center students in their learning experiences?
2. Another key idea in this chapter is that grammar inquiries move grammar instruction from asset-based to deficit-based. Why do you think asset-based grammar instruction is important?

3. The chapter also describes how inquiry- and asset-based grammar instruction incorporates the power of essential questions. Based on what you've read in this book and any other experience you have with the topic, why do you think essential questions can be powerful for students' learning experiences?
4. Finally, the chapter explains that grammar inquiries prepare students for authentic engagement with language. Why do you think it is important for students to look at examples of grammatical concepts that they encounter in their everyday lives?
5. What is something from your experience reading and reflection on inquiry- and asset-based grammar instruction that has stood out to you? How will this approach impact teaching and learning in your classroom?

Appendix B

Reproducible Charts and Forms to Use in Your Classroom

This appendix contains reproducible charts and forms aligned with the instructional practices discussed in this book. These resources will help you implement the methods of inquiry-based grammar instruction described throughout the book's chapters.

Focal Grammatical Concept	Mentor Text Title	Excerpt from the Text	Why the Focal Concept is Important to the Effectiveness of the Text

Figure 1.2 Mentor Text Analysis Graphic Organizer

Authentic Example of Focal Grammatical Concept	Think-Aloud Points About its Features You'll Share with Students	Another Example of the Grammatical Concept	Students' Insights Regardings its Features

Figure 2.2 Graphic Organizer: Examples and Features of Grammatical Concepts

Copyright material from Sean Ruday (2023), *Grammar Inquiries, Grades 6–12*, Routledge

Reflection Questions	Statements from Student Observations	Summary Points to Share with Students
Why do you think the creator of the text used this example of the grammatical concept?		
How do you think the text would be different if the grammatical concept was not used?		

Figure 3.1 Grammatical Concept Discussion Graphic Organizer

Grammatical Concept Example	Context In Which It Was Used	Why the Text's Creator May Have Used the Concept	How the Text Would Be Different If the Concept Was Not Used

Figure 4.1 Grammatical Concept Analysis Graphic Organizer

Copyright material from Sean Ruday (2023), *Grammar Inquiries, Grades 6–12*, Routledge

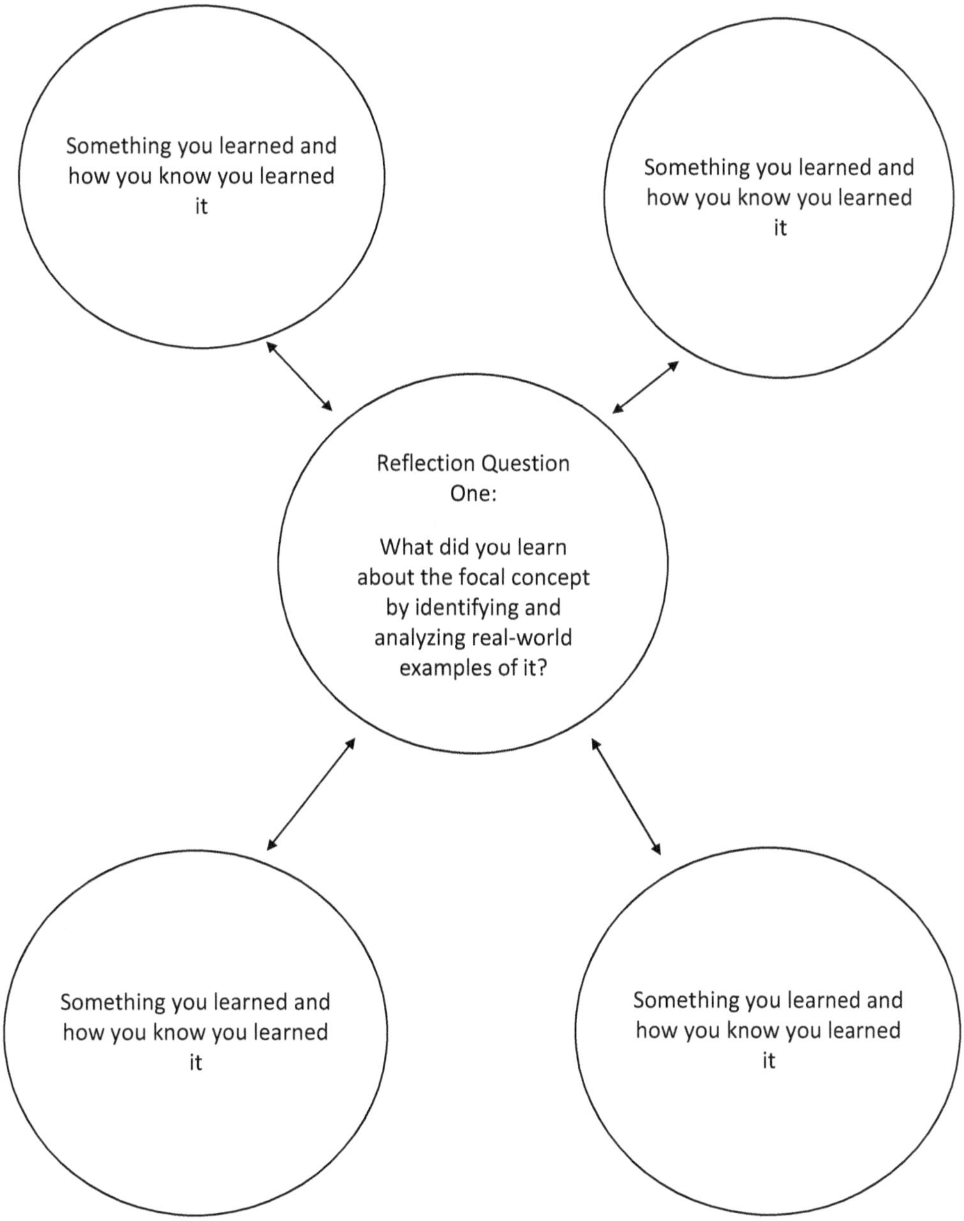

Something you learned and how you know you learned it

Something you learned and how you know you learned it

Reflection Question One:

What did you learn about the focal concept by identifying and analyzing real-world examples of it?

Something you learned and how you know you learned it

Something you learned and how you know you learned it

Figure 6.3 Reflection Question One Brainstorm Template

Copyright material from Sean Ruday (2023), *Grammar Inquiries, Grades 6–12*, Routledge

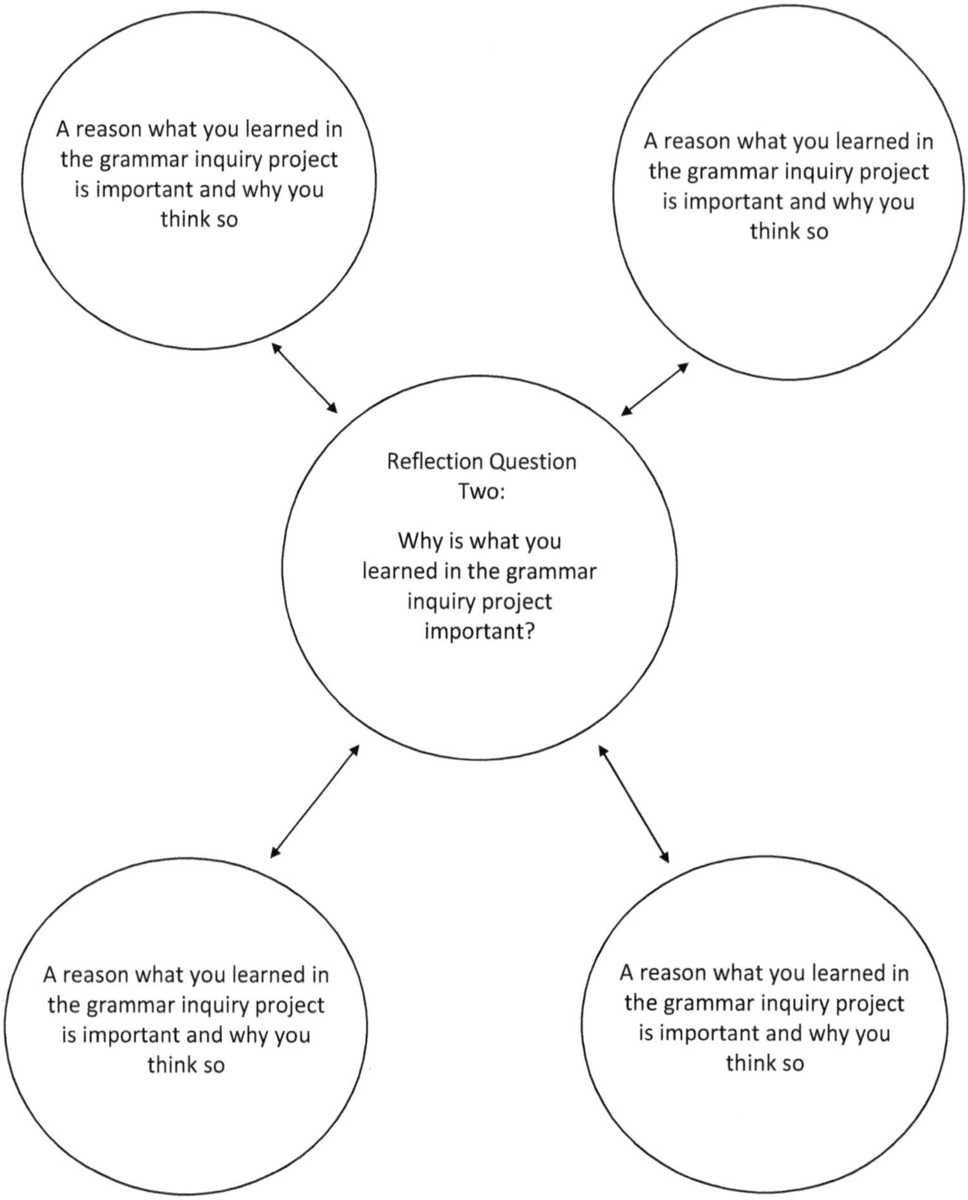

A reason what you learned in the grammar inquiry project is important and why you think so

A reason what you learned in the grammar inquiry project is important and why you think so

Reflection Question Two:

Why is what you learned in the grammar inquiry project important?

A reason what you learned in the grammar inquiry project is important and why you think so

A reason what you learned in the grammar inquiry project is important and why you think so

Figure 6.4 Reflection Question Two Brainstorm Template

Copyright material from Sean Ruday (2023), *Grammar Inquiries, Grades 6–12*, Routledge

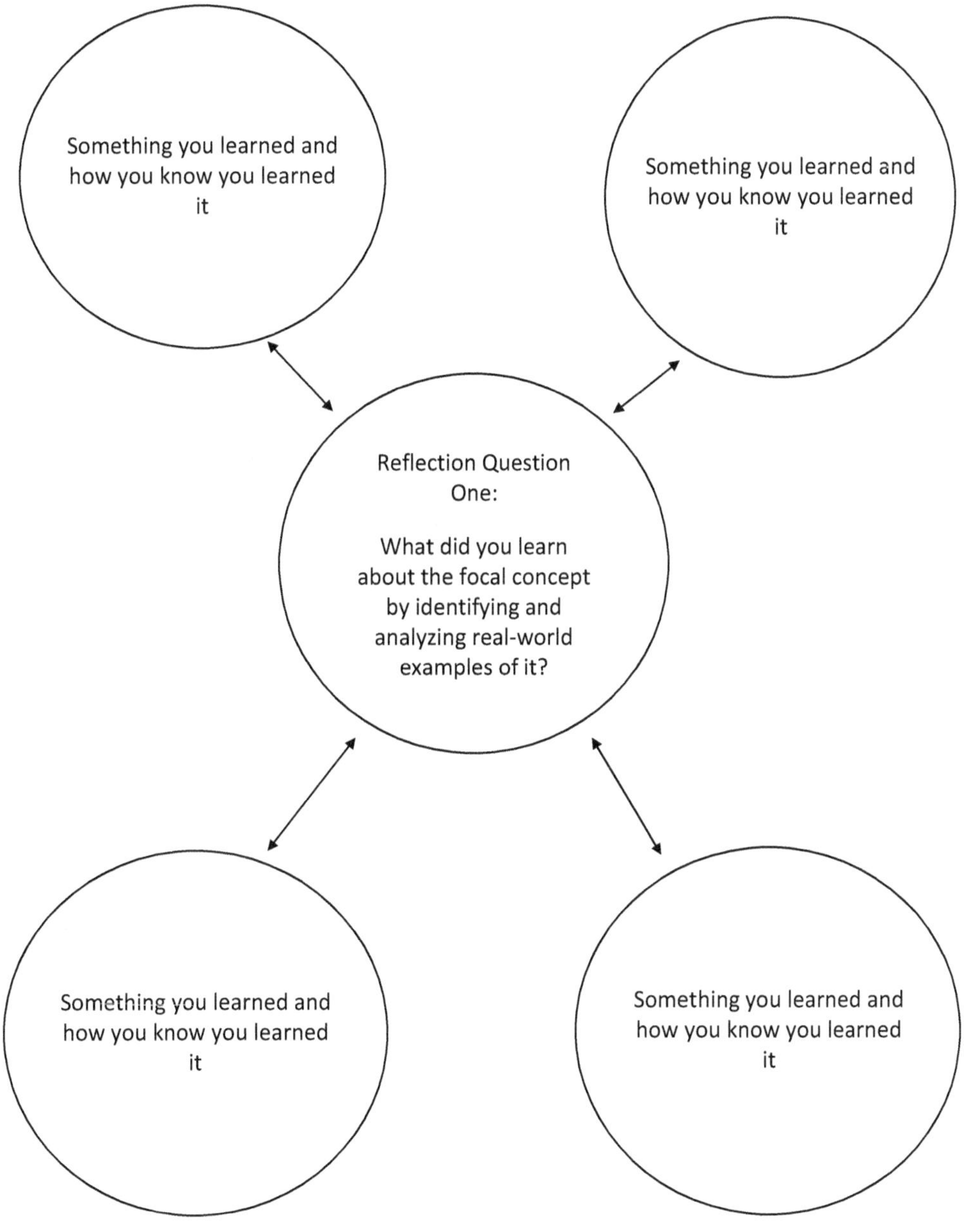

- Something you learned and how you know you learned it
- Something you learned and how you know you learned it

Reflection Question One:

What did you learn about the focal concept by identifying and analyzing real-world examples of it?

- Something you learned and how you know you learned it
- Something you learned and how you know you learned it

Figure 6.3 Reflection Question One Brainstorm Template

Copyright material from Sean Ruday (2023), *Grammar Inquiries, Grades 6–12*, Routledge

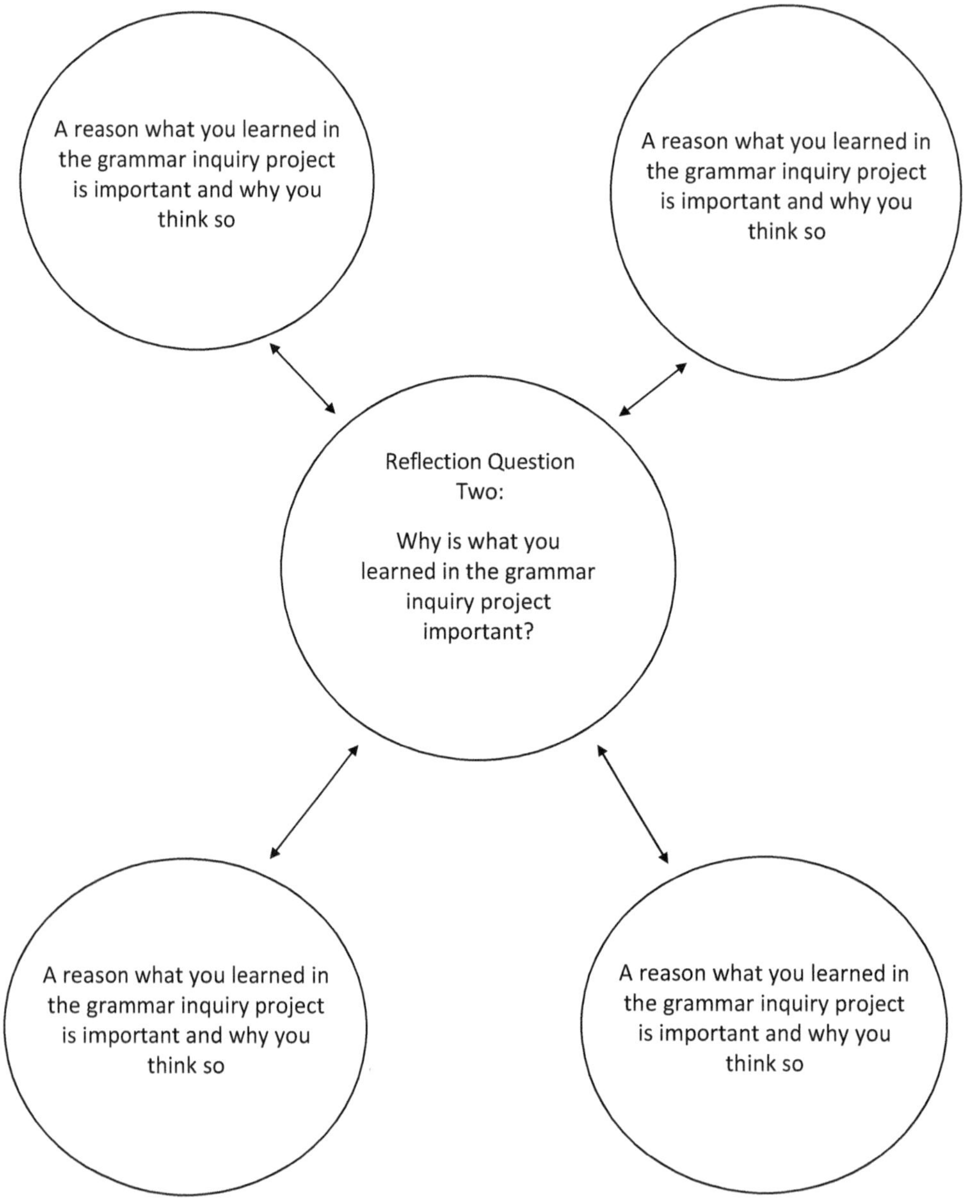

```
┌─────────────────────┐                    ┌─────────────────────┐
│ A reason what you   │                    │ A reason what you   │
│ learned in the      │                    │ learned in the      │
│ grammar inquiry     │                    │ grammar inquiry     │
│ project is important│                    │ project is important│
│ and why you think so│                    │ and why you think so│
└─────────────────────┘                    └─────────────────────┘
            ↕                                          ↕
                    ┌─────────────────────┐
                    │ Reflection Question │
                    │        Two:         │
                    │                     │
                    │  Why is what you    │
                    │ learned in the      │
                    │ grammar inquiry     │
                    │ project important?  │
                    └─────────────────────┘
            ↕                                          ↕
┌─────────────────────┐                    ┌─────────────────────┐
│ A reason what you   │                    │ A reason what you   │
│ learned in the      │                    │ learned in the      │
│ grammar inquiry     │                    │ grammar inquiry     │
│ project is important│                    │ project is important│
│ and why you think so│                    │ and why you think so│
└─────────────────────┘                    └─────────────────────┘
```

Figure 6.4 Reflection Question Two Brainstorm Template

Copyright material from Sean Ruday (2023), *Grammar Inquiries, Grades 6–12*, Routledge

Areas of Improvement	Criteria	Strengths
	The presentation is three to five minutes long and stays on topic throughout. Score:_____/5	
	The presentation slides include a combination of text and relevant images. Score:_____/5	
	The presentation content relates to the grammar inquiry's essential question. Score:_____/5	
	The presentation identifies an authentic example of the focal concept that the presenter found. Score:_____/5	
	The presentation contains a thoughtful analysis of the identified example that discusses why the text's creator may have used the focal concept and how the text would be different without it. Score: _____/5	
	The presentation contains a concluding section that clearly connects the identification and analysis with the essential question Score:_____/5	

Figure 7.1 Grammar Inquiry Rubric

(*Continued*)

Copyright material from Sean Ruday (2023), *Grammar Inquiries, Grades 6–12*, Routledge

	The answer to each reflection question is approximately one paragraph long and stays on topic throughout.	
	Score:_____/5	
	The answer to each question reveals thoughtful ideas and careful reflections regarding that question. Score:_____/5	
	The ideas in the responses are supported by specific examples and details from the writer's own grammar inquiries. Score:_____/5	

Total score:_____/45

Percentage:

Comments:

Figure 7.1 (Continued)

For Product Safety Concerns and Information please contact our EU representative GPSR@taylorandfrancis.com
Taylor & Francis Verlag GmbH, Kaufingerstraße 24, 80331 München, Germany

www.ingramcontent.com/pod-product-compliance
Lightning Source LLC
Chambersburg PA
CBHW060514300426
44112CB00017B/2663